FAITH, HOPE, LOVE AND LAUGHTER

PAUL KRAUS was born in Austria in 1944 and came to Australia as a young child. He studied at the Conservatorium of Music and then gained a B.A. from Macquarie University. He later completed postgraduate studies at the University of Sydney in History and Education. He has been a history teacher for most of his life and has written several books on Australian history. He currently works as a freelance writer and journalist and lives on the New South Wales coast.

The great error in the treatment of the human body is that physicians are ignorant of the whole. For the part can never be well unless the whole is well.

Plato

There are only two ways to live your life. One is as though nothing is a miracle. The other is as though everything is a miracle.

Albert Einstein

FAITH, HOPE, LOVE AND LAUGHTER

HOW THEY HEAL

Edited by

Paul Kraus

First published in 1999

Typeset by
Midland Typesetters Pty Ltd
Maryborough, Victoria 3465

Printed and bound by
Australian Print Group
Maryborough, Victoria 3465

For the publisher
Hale & Iremonger Pty Ltd
PO Box 205, Alexandria, NSW 2015

National Library of Australia
Cataloguing-in-Publication entry:

Faith, hope, love & laughter: how they heal.

ISBN 0 86806 683 4.

1. Holistic medicine. 2. Healing - Philosophy. 3. Mental healing. I. Kraus, Paul, 1944- .

613

CONTENTS

7

I dedicate this book to my wife, Sue, whose love, encouragement and deep self-sacrifice has been such a powerful healing force in my life; my mother, for her loving kindness and never-failing generosity, especially with the financial help for expensive therapies; David and Nicholas, for being two wonderful sons; Dr Peter Spitzer, who right from the beginning pointed me towards a healing path and helped me stay on it; Ian Gawler, who taught me so much about maintaining wellness and who told me to accept the diagnosis, but to ignore the prognosis; Professor Avni Sali and Dr John Piesse, both truly holistic doctors, whose encouragement and advice has been a strong impetus to staying well; Col Douglass for teaching me so much about generosity; and the Cancer Support Association of Western Australia in Cottesloe, Perth, for providing strong inspiration and hope at a time when I really needed it.

PREFACE

Science would have us believe that healing is a rational business, that it is possible to analyse the elements behind why some people heal and others do not. In the field of cancer, scientific medicine certainly has a lot to offer. Surgery has a mechanical precision to it that is highly predictable and reliable in controlled circumstances. Perhaps chemotherapy and radiotherapy are somewhat less defined in their mode of action and predictability of outcome. Therapies based on the immune system appear to be more experimental and, while offering great promise, still would appear to be in the infant stages of development. Even more so, considering the metabolism of the cancer cell and how it might be modulated to affect the growth and the healing of cancer is brave new territory.

Yet clearly above and beyond all these obvious issues, lies the realm of the human spirit with its own incredible potentials. It seems that if we limit our possibilities to what is purely scientific, we limit ourselves to what can be rationalised, analysed, broken into smaller pieces and looked at under a microscope. Useful as this may be, it is clear that the really important things in life do not respond to such analysis.

Major principles which deeply touch the human condition are faith, hope and love. Each of these principles is essentially mysterious. Mysterious in that they can not be fully accounted for by logic or reason. This is not to say that they are illogical, it is only to say that they go beyond logic; that they exist in a part of our being that is beyond the thinking mind, that they are essentially non-rational.

To be touched by faith, hope or love is to be touched by the mysterious. This is a direct experience. It is inevitably a heartfelt experience, an experience of soul-like quality. When we are touched in this way there comes a deep abiding calm, a profound sense of inner peace. What this experience often leads to could be called radical healing. Radical in the sense that it is *fundamental*, profound and lasting. This radical healing can exist independently of physical healing, although it is highly likely to be accompanied by profound and often remarkable physical healing. It would seem to be what true healing is about: the reconnection with the heart, the reconnection with the soul, the reconnection with the spirit.

So how to be touched by this radical healing? Clearly the answer has to be to be touched by faith, hope and love. Paul Kraus is one of those remarkable cancer survivors who has been touched in this way. It is obvious in his way of being. Inspired by this experience, granted to him like some extraordinary compensatory gift for the trauma of major illness, Paul has collected an amazing anthology of inspiring writings. These include wonderful extracts from many great writers and from his own poetic commentaries, all of which seek to convey something of the mystery of faith, hope, laughter and radical healing.

My own hope is that in reading all this you too will be opened to and touched by these fundamental and profound mysteries of life.

Dr Ian Gawler OAM BVSc

FOREWORD

Paul Kraus knows first-hand the kaleidoscope of feelings that present themselves whilst travelling along the cancer diagnosis road. Healing can take place at a variety of levels and it is the experience of faith, hope, love and laughter that helps to open the door to that place of healing.

The Clown Doctors of The Humour Foundation aim to bring joy and laughter to sick children in hospital. The vehicle for this includes improvisation, music, mime, story-telling, and parodying medical procedures, such as our famous red-nose transplant. Our regular visits change the feeling in the ward and as the relationship with the children, staff and parents develops, we all become richer for the experience.

Go ahead, open the door.

Dr Peter Spitzer (aka Dr Fruit-Loop)
Chairman and Medical Director
The Humour Foundation

INTRODUCTION

Many years ago I read on a church noticeboard: 'Life is fragile—handle with prayer'. Whatever our belief system may be, everyone would agree that life is unpredictable and that illness is not the sole preserve of old age. Children, adolescents and those in the prime of life succumb (with increasing frequency) to life-threatening illnesses. Yet, it seems that only when we are personally touched by illness do we stop to think about the fact that life and health are precious possessions.

It is not only illness that can play havoc with our lives. Other life crises have similar effects: a broken relationship, bereavement, unemployment, the serious illness of a loved one, fear of the future, or merely the fear of ageing. Unlike a life-threatening illness, which is not so commonly experienced, there would be few people who reach middle age without having been subjected to the psychological and emotional (if not indeed the physical) ravages of one or more of these traumas.

All of these events and situations involve personal suffering— from which none of us is immune. They affect each level of existence: body, mind and spirit. Some people, particularly those with healthy immune systems, are able to withstand a life crisis without succumbing to illness, while others become sick.

In ancient Greece, doctors worked under the patronage of Aesculapius, the god of medicine. They believed that the chief role of the physician was to treat disease, to restore health by correcting any imperfections caused by accidents of birth or life. In Greek mythology Aesculapius's daughter was Hygeia, the radiant goddess of health. Those who worshipped Hygeia believed that health is the natural order of things. Further, it was believed that all people were entitled to health—providing they govern their lives according to certain natural laws which ensure that a person has a healthy mind in a healthy body.

Essentially, modern Western medicine has followed the philosophy of Aesculapius. We have clear expectations of our doctors—to provide a cure for our illness, but few of us realise that curing our symptoms does not necessarily equate with healing. That is why, so often, our illness returns. Within modern medicine an ever-increasing number of doctors are drawing our attention to the importance of preventative medicine: to the fact that illness could be minimised if our lives were more balanced. Very frequently, illness is the body's warning system reminding us that the balance has been upset.

This anthology of poems, short stories and writings is about the ways in which faith, hope, love and laughter promote health and healing. I have deliberately chosen to include poetry because of its direct appeal to our emotions. The American poet Carl Sandburg has described poetry as 'a search for syllables to shoot at the barriers of the unknown and the unknowable' or 'as a series of explanations of life, fading into horizons too swift for explanations'. Poetry is the most concentrated form of language and, as such, conveys its message powerfully and succinctly.

Some of the poems and short stories are the direct result of my own cancer diagnosis in June 1997. The prose extracts (excluding the short stories) are a distillation of some of the finest writings about health and healing, from a holistic viewpoint, in recent decades.

Paradoxically, my cancer diagnosis has come with a hidden blessing. My illness has forced me to review life's priorities and agendas. It has been a powerful stimulus in making major changes in my life. It has also starkly challenged, and strengthened, my faith in God. In doing this, my illness has deeply enriched my spiritual pilgrimage. I have become much more sensitive to the way I relate to my fellow human beings. I have come to appreciate just how much love and compassion has been shown

13

to me in my hour of need and I have come to realise how very easy it is to be self-centred and to forget the needs of others.

I do not know what impact this diagnosis has on my lease of life but I do have the tremendous assurance that God's love is deep and unconditional, whatever the future may hold. I have gained a certainty about the fact that this often-times puzzling tapestry of our existence has a broader context than our 'three score years and ten'.

I have come to realise that any setback, cancer or any other illness or misfortunate can be viewed in a positive way and can be a means of personal growth. I count this as a blessing. A further blessing is the realisation that whatever my situation in life, ultimately, when I come to the end of my days, the only thing that will have mattered is how much love I have brought into the world.

This collection of writings aims to focus our attention on 'ultimate realities', those things in life which really matter; on those things which actively promote a sense of well-being, and on those things which help us to live more fulfilling lives.

Sometimes it is only when a life crisis such as illness occurs that we are forced into a situation of self-awareness which in turn, gives us the opportunity to grow, to find inner peace and to live a more meaningful existence—a life in which faith, hope, love, peace and joy expand our horizons.

Dr Bernie Siegel, an American surgeon who has a deep interest in mind–body medicine, has written:

We must all confront the reality that no-one lives forever. Illness and death are not signs of failure; what is a failure is not living. Our goal is learning to live—joyously and lovingly. Disease can often teach us to do that.

The poems, short stories and extracts found in this book are all life-affirming in that they deal with the attainment of inner peace, health and healing. Indeed, they are intended as signposts of healing—physical or spiritual. They deal with the great common denominator of our existence—our spirituality; our inner being; our soul. If we are to experience healing, either physical or emotional, it must come from within, beginning with having peace of mind and with living in the moment; with having balance in our lives.

These attributes of wellness also come from having a right relationship with our God and with each other. Only then will those great enemies of good health—bitterness, guilt, anger and resentment—subside. This is one of the great themes of the Book of Psalms in the Bible. The writers of this book pondered the meaning of their lives in relation to the infinite wisdom and order in the universe which their God had created. All of us have some kind of god in our lives, albeit, frequently the god we follow is something as tenuous as career or money. By definition, material comforts are incapable of bringing inner peace, which is a searching of the spirit. Our capacity to live balanced and, therefore, healthy lives, is to a large extent determined by what kind of god guides us.

I believe passionately that faith, hope, love and laughter are very powerful healers, especially love.

The American poet Emily Dickinson wrote so poignantly about hope as an enduring quality:

Hope is the thing with feathers
That perches in the soul,
And sings the tune without the words,
And never stops at all.

Likewise, as the extracts in this book attempt to show, laughter enhances our quality of life by releasing stress and energising our body and mind. It does this by lifting our mood through a complex interaction between endorphin receptors and neuro-peptides. Very simply, laughter has been shown through scientific investigation to favourably alter the biochemical reactions in the body. Scientists tell us that these biochemical reactions also have a positive effect on the body's defence mechanism, commonly known as the immune system.

The proceeds of sales from this anthology on healing are directed to the 'Clown Doctors', who form the Humour

Foundation of Australia. Dr Peter Spitzer of Bowral, New South Wales, established The Foundation in January 1997 with a unit at the Children's Hospital, Randwick, in Sydney. Since that time a unit has been established at the Royal Children's Hospital in Melbourne. More units are planned at the New Children's Hospital at Westmead in Sydney and elsewhere. Hopefully, the Clown Doctors will be a feature of all major hospitals across Australia in the next few years. The overall aim of the Foundation is to bring laughter and healing to sick children in hospital, as well as to those who care for them—hospital staff and parents.

The angels must rejoice each time Peter and his growing number of Clown Doctors across Australia bring a smile to the face of a sick and suffering child.

'Blessed are the peacemakers, for they shall be called children of God.'

Paul Kraus

FAITH AND HOPE

Faith, Hope and Love—The Perfect Healers

LORD, make me an instrument of your peace.
Where there is hatred, let me sow love.
Where there is injury, pardon.
Where there is doubt, faith.
Where there is despair, hope.
Where there is darkness, light,
And where there is sadness, joy.

O Divine Master, grant that I may not
so much seek to be consoled, as to console;
to be understood, as to understand;
to be loved, as to love;
for it is in giving that we receive,
it is in pardoning that we are pardoned,
and it is in dying that we are born to eternal life.

St Francis of Assisi

The Four Faiths

We have found that four faiths are crucial to recovering from serious illness: faith in oneself, one's doctor, one's treatment, and one's spiritual faith. The last, although seldom totally achievable by most of us, is in many ways a key to the others.

The 'spiritual life' has many meanings. It need not be reflected in any commitment to organised religion, and we all know that some of the most outwardly pious people are the least spiritual. These are the ones who give other people 'spiritual ulcers'. From the standpoint of a healer, I view spirituality as including the belief in some meaning and order in the universe. I view the force behind creation as a loving, intelligent energy. For some, this is labelled God, for others, it can be seen simply as a source of healing. From this comes the ability to find peace, to resolve the apparent contradictions between one's emotions and reality, between internal and external.

Spirituality means acceptance of what is (not to be confused with resignation or approval of evil). Jesus told us to love our enemies, not like them and not have no enemies. In an abandoned, bombed-out house in Germany at the end of World War II, Allied soldiers found a testimony to this faith scratched into a basement wall by one of the victims of the Holocaust:

I believe in the sun—even when it does not shine;
I believe in love—even when it is not shown;
I believe in God—even when he does not speak.

Spirituality means the ability to find peace and happiness in an imperfect world, and to feel that one's own personality is imperfect but acceptable. From this peaceful state of mind come both creativity and the ability to love unselfishly, which go hand in hand. Acceptance, faith, forgiveness, peace and love are the traits that define spirituality for me. These characteristics *always* appear in those who achieve unexpected healing from serious illness ... A person who believes in a benevolent higher power has a potent reason for hope—and hope is physiologic ...

Those who profess a faith merely because their parents did

or because it increases their social standing are unlikely to really believe it can heal them. Sometimes religion even becomes a negative factor. People think, 'If God gave me this illness, who am I to get well?' Beliefs that lean heavily on guilt, original sin, and predestination are of little use for healing. By the same token, it's hard to find peace in life if you believe death is a meaningless end or earthly existence is futile. That's why I prefer to speak of spirituality rather than religion, to avoid doctrinal limitations ...

I think of God as the same potential healing force—an intelligent, loving energy or light—in each person's life ... I suggest that patients think of illness not as God's will but as our deviation from God's will. To me it is the absence of spirituality that leads to difficulties ...

The energy of hope and faith is always available. We all must die someday, but the spiritual way is always open to everyone and can make our lives beautiful whenever we choose it. As the German dramatist Christian Friedrich Hebbel once wrote, 'Life is not anything, it is only the opportunity for something'.

Extract taken from Love, Medicine and Miracles
by Bernie Siegel, MD
Used with the permission of the publisher,
Arrow Books, London.

The Good Patient

He was the most unusual patient I have ever treated. 'Unusual' is probably the wrong word. He was quite extraordinary. Extraordinary in the sense that he made me reconsider my notions of healing. Helmut was a catalyst—setting me thinking about complementary and holistic medicine. It was about seven years ago that I made his acquaintance, when he first became my patient, shortly after he and his wife arrived in North Queensland.

Helmut was one of those quaint characters who float to the top of Australia from the southern states. I had only just joined the practice when he presented one morning. In his early thirties and a picture of health: broad-shouldered, bronzed by the tropical sun and always wearing a battered broad-brimmed hat. I knew who he was the moment I walked into the surgery.

He had become one of the 'local identities' in the few years he had lived in the area. A week earlier the local newspaper featured an article about Helmut Schmidt being commissioned to carve a statue for the Catholic Cathedral in Cairns. An enormously gifted woodturner, he had learned his craft in Germany from where he had migrated. Apart from being a master craftsman, he was also a fine violinist. His wife, Heidi, was a candle-maker. She manned a craft stall at the local markets, as well as selling her beautiful wares to gift shops in the district. Except for being seen at the fortnightly local markets, the couple kept to themselves. They lived on a small property just outside town with two sheep, a cow, a few chickens, a dog and a cat.

'How can I help you, Helmut?' I asked.

'For this kind of nuisance, I don't really have the time. Let me show you the problem, *ja?*'

Within an instant Helmut had discarded his shirt. Before he had time to speak, I saw exactly what his problem was.

'Mmm, I can tell you immediately that your problem is an umbilical hernia. Nevertheless, hop up on the couch and I will have a closer look. Probably from all the lifting that comes with your work.'

'Yes, doctor, you are quite right. In Germany a few years ago I had to have a hernia operation. Since then I am always very careful when I lift ... obviously, not careful enough. Now, doctor, I suppose you will tell me that I need surgery ... *ja?*'

'I'm afraid so, Helmut. There's simply no other way of fixing this problem.' Helmut sighed deeply.

'*Mein Gott* ... I'm so busy. This is not urgent, is it, doctor?'

'It's not urgent, but I guess it's not advisable to leave things too long. As with any problem if left for too long, it will only get worse. Would you like me to write you a referral?'

Helmut again sighed in resignation, 'I suppose you better, doctor.'

'Are you in a private health fund, Helmut?'

'No, doctor. Neither of us ever go near to a doctor since we came to Australia.'

'In that case, you realise that it would probably take some months for you to be treated. There is quite a lengthy waiting list for non-urgent cases like yours.'

'Oh, that's fine ... all the better ... I'm so terribly busy for at least the next couple of months.'

'Well, that's alright, Helmut, but I do suggest you go and see the surgeon as soon as possible so that you can be put on the hospital waiting list.'

'I will do as you say, doctor,' Helmut said with quiet resignation.

I wrote the referral and handed it to him. That was the last I heard from him for six months.

Late one afternoon, just as the last patient was leaving, a call came through from Dr Walker, the surgeon to whom I had referred Helmut. It was a call that left me stunned. Dr Walker had operated on Helmut earlier that day to repair his hernia. In the course of the procedure he discovered an unusual amount of fluid in his abdominal cavity. A laproscopic examination was performed which revealed wide-spread tumours—metastases throughout the peritoneal cavity. Dr Walker unsuccessfully tried to find the primary tumour. His training led him to the belief that it was located in the pancreas, particularly because the patient had not complained of any adverse symptoms. Samples were already at the pathologist for biopsy. Based on the widespread extent of the tumours the prognosis was not at all good—perhaps six months. Helmut and his wife had already been informed of the unfortunate news that afternoon.

Two days later Helmut and Heidi came to see me. I spotted them sitting in a corner of the rather crowded waiting room. Their presence unsettled me. I felt so inadequate. What on earth *could* I say which would give them reassurance or hope? I really had no time to rehearse my spiel. No time to think of positive things to say. How could I ameliorate the gloomy prognosis they had been given? Helplessness gave way to guilt and self-recrimination. Why wasn't I more thorough when he came for that initial consultation? No, stop with such stupid self-blame. There was simply nothing, absolutely nothing to warrant further investigation. While self-justification wiped away my guilt, I was still left with the conundrum of what to say.

They sat down alongside my desk. Helmut was expressionless; Heidi ashen-faced. A brief silence. I sighed softly as I opened Helmut's file and retrieved Dr Walker's letter. I groped for meaningful words. Words which might somehow transcend the obvious. They're vulnerable. I could only guess how shocked they must be feeling. This situation again reminded me how inadequate my long years of training had been to equip me to communicate effectively in times of difficulty or a crisis such as this.

'Well, well, well, Helmut. This certainly is a nasty surprise ... a *very* nasty surprise. I could hardly believe what Dr Walker told me the other day. Tell me, Helmut, did you have *any* abnormal symptoms lately? Anything that could have made you suspicious that something was wrong?'

Helmut momentarily paused, frowned, shook his head and shrugged his shoulders, 'No, nothing. I can't think of anything beyond regular mild indigestion and a tendency to ... how you call it? ... bloat? Is that the word?'

'Yes, but Helmut, that's a problem you share with the majority of the population. There's nothing unusual about the symptoms you mention.'

Heidi spoke: 'Doctor, he has been taking herbs and digestive enzymes for a number of years . . . as long as I can remember, he has had trouble with his digestion . . . but nothing has prepared us for this . . . we simply can't believe it . . . we think it is important to have a second opinion. Maybe this doctor has made a terrible mistake . . .'

'I would also like to think so, Mrs Schmidt. If you want a second opinion I can certainly arrange that, but let's take one step at a time. I realise that it must be very difficult, but we really must wait for a few days to see what the pathologist's report shows. It is most important that we get an accurate and definite diagnosis. As soon as we have that I would like to see you both again and we can talk about a plan of action.'

'If we must wait for the pathology for a definite diagnosis, then, *Mein Gott*, why he give me such terrible news before he had all the results. This I don't understand.'

'The only thing I can say in Dr Walker's defence is that he got such a shock from his discovery that he felt he must tell you about it . . . remember, he has seen tumours like this many, many times. Based on his observations he believed he recognised the type of tumours he saw. Of course, he realised immediately the need to get confirmation of his discovery.'

My heart went out to this bewildered couple sitting alongside me. I felt that anything I said sounded academic and trite—of little comfort.

'Has the social worker from the hospital spoken to you about this diagnosis?'

'No, no-one at all,' replied Heidi.

A wave of indignation welled up within me. Extreme carelessness on the Matron's part not to have immediately followed up Helmut's case. 'Would either of you like to speak with her?'

They looked briefly—and rather blankly—at each other and then courteously denied the offer. A brief awkward silence followed. Heidi sat there shaking her head. Suddenly she burst into tears. Helmut put his arms around her and made comforting noises. Professional detachment pushed its limits. The lump in

25

my throat was painful. When she had recomposed herself, I turned to them and said, 'At this stage, it's difficult for me to say much more. Make an appointment for the end of the week when we have the pathology results and we'll plan a course of action. In the meantime what I would advise you is this: Accept the diagnosis, but firmly reject the prognosis. Any doctor can only go on statistics in making any prediction about a disease. Statistics don't take into account the uniqueness of each patient—they only consider the disease itself. There is so much you can do to put yourself on the right side of the statistics. So—take heart! Remember, that whatever diagnosis the pathology comes up with, there *are* things we can do about it! There *are* treatments available. The most important thing is to retain a positive outlook—to be aware that *any* illness can be overcome.'

A few days later Helmut and Heidi were back. Despite their ordeal, I was surprised at how well they looked. They seemed much calmer than on the previous visit.

'The pathology report is really what Dr Walker had expected. It is what we call an adenocarcinoma.' Dr Walker's observations had proven to be correct. The CT scan showed widespread metastatic (cancerous) spread throughout the abdominal lining. 'I would strongly suggest that you go and see an oncologist, Helmut, to determine the most appropriate course of treatment. This is not my field.'

They nodded. I wrote the referral, folded the page, put it into a sealed envelope and handed it to Helmut.

'Before you go, I would like you to have a blood test, so that you could take the results with you to the specialist.' Helmut nodded in consent. Again I tried to find some words of encouragement, especially pointing out that Helmut's strong creativity was a powerful incentive to keep positive. Creativity, like faith and hope, laughter and music, uplifts the soul and is a strong inducement to good health.

Almost a fortnight went by before I saw Helmut again. In the meantime his blood test results came back. I was very pleasantly surprised. His full blood count was near perfect: liver function normal, red cell morphology, white cell differential all

OK. The biggest surprise of all, and very encouraging—was that his cancer tumour markers were also normal. Helmut's report from the oncologist hadn't arrived by the time he came to see me.

This time he came on his own. He looked well, in spite of everything.

'What's been happening? How are you feeling?'

'Not too bad at all, thanks doctor.'

'You certainly are looking very well . . . and that's so important. And how is your wife?'

'Much better than when you saw her, doctor.'

'And how did your visit to the oncologist go? I haven't heard from him yet.'

'Not too well . . . I didn't like his attitude. Sure, he was thorough. He examined me, asked me many questions, studied the scans and asked me to have another blood test.'

'What didn't you like about his attitude, Helmut?'

'He offered me no words of hope. He had a negativity about him and he didn't like it when I continued asking him the questions I had prepared. He was—what you call it—"straight down the line." Start with heavy doses of chemotherapy treatment; that's OK—he's the specialist, but when I asked him about other things I could do which might help, he simply handed me a booklet from the Cancer Council. He is not a good communicator.'

'How did your wife feel about the consultation?'

'She felt frustrated and angry by his apparent lack of concern . . . by his clinical detachment. She felt that he might be a good doctor, but she wonders how he can be a good healer when he doesn't listen carefully to his patients. Furthermore, she was worried about the oncologist saying that the success rate with the chemotherapy is not so high . . . not even 50%. She wants to try other things.'

'What other things?' I asked.

'Vitamins, minerals and herbs which specifically have anti-cancer properties . . . iscador, or mistletoe injections and maybe even intravenous vitamin C to raise the immune function.'

27

I sighed in mild exasperation. Likeable though he was, Helmut was testing my patience talking such mumbo-jumbo in the face of such a serious diagnosis. I suppressed my indignation by suggesting that he might consider having a second oncological opinion. 'Helmut, the decision about your treatment is one that only you can make. You might want to have a second opinion. The important thing is to arrive at a course of treatment and then confidently go with it. Research has shown that cancer patients who have a strong belief that their treament is working, generally have better outcomes and have more success with their treatment . . . the self-fulfilling prophecy, so to speak.'

'You mentioned a second opinion. Actually, I already have had a second medical opinion, although not from an oncologist.'

I looked at him in surprise, 'From whom?'

'I have a friend in Cairns who is a natural therapist. He was trained as a doctor in Germany but does not practise here in Australia. Back in Germany he has treated hundreds of cancer patients. I had a long consultation with him the other day. He gave us much hope.'

'In what way, Helmut?'

'He studied my file and then told me that *any* type of cancer can be cured. Our state of mind is such an important factor in determining the course of the disease. For various reasons he was not in favour of chemotherapy . . .'

'But Helmut, you must remember that your natural therapist is not an oncologist. He simply does not have the expertise of an oncologist. I would be very wary of taking the advice of anyone other than an oncologist if I was in your situation. At any rate, what did he recommend?'

'He gave me two different types of herbs to take. One is specifically to build up the immune system; the other is to inhibit the spread of the tumours. He also recommended a special anti-cancer diet which includes drinking vegetable juices, especially carrots, with their high betacarotene content. He urged me to increase my meditating and to cut back on my work, to avoid stress.'

'Helmut, you do realise that in this country a naturopath, or natural therapist is not allowed by law to treat cancer?'

'Doctor, let me explain that my friend, Dr Hutter, is not specifically treating the cancer; he is working on building my immune system, so that my body can fight the cancer. I believe that when the immune system is strong, we have a better chance to fight this illness.'

Frustration was setting in. My patience was wearing thin. I could only hold my tongue for so long while listening to this simplistic nonsense. I felt obliged to tell him that he was playing a very chancy game in the face of this serious diagnosis. Doesn't he realise that widespread metastases is virtually synonymous with a death sentence? 'Remember, Helmut, that last time you were here I suggested that it might be an idea for you to have a second opinion as to which treatment would be the most effective. Unfortunately, Helmut, what you are currently doing does not have any—or at least, very little—scientific evidence to show its effectiveness. What you should be doing is making sure that you give yourself the optimal chance to survive your illness. At the moment I don't believe you're doing that.'

Helmut sat there impassively. After a few moment's silence he spoke, 'Alright, doctor, I am happy to have a second opinion ... I agree with you, I want to find out the best treatment ... at the same time, doctor, I am convinced that if only we give our body the chance to heal, it will, whatever the disease.'

More nonsense fed to him by his naturopathic friend. I felt annoyed to think about these self-styled 'healers,' these charlatans who prey on the vulnerable for their own profit. 'Would you like me to write you a referral to see another oncologist? I mean, it's entirely up to you, Helmut. If you would rather not, then that's fine with me.'

'That would be a good idea ... ja ... thank you doctor, I will go for a second opinion.'

'I think it would be interesting to get his opinion. The doctor I am sending you to has an outstanding reputation. What he doesn't know about cancer is really not worth knowing. I'll write

29

his details on the front of the envelope. Give his secretary a ring and make a time.'

I wrote Helmut the referral and wished him well. A few weeks later I received the report from the oncologist:

'Thank you for referring Mr Schmidt to me . . . the accidental discovery of Mr Schmidt's cancer was an amazing find . . . I had a long talk to Mr Schmidt and his wife. I explained to them the nature of his type of cancer. I told them that without chemotherapy his outlook did not look very promising . . . his survival would then be in months rather than years. I recommended that he start a course of chemotherapy as soon as possible. Unfortunately, Mr Schmidt was reluctant—indeed, for the time being, he refused to accept such a course of treatment . . . for the present, he has opted for alternate treatment from Germany. I told them both that should they want to see me at any time, I would be glad to do so.'

I shook my head. On the one hand, Helmut is a highly intelligent, gifted young man; on the other, he is so gullible. He seems intent on playing a very chancy game. I feared for his outlook. The longer he postponed treatment, the dimmer his survival prospects.

About nine months passed. Sheer pressure of work allowed Helmut's case to recede from my thoughts, although there had been reminders which made me wonder how he was getting along. Then, one evening, standing in a supermarket queue, lost in my own thoughts, I heard from behind a softly-spoken female voice with a distinctly German accent call: 'Hello, doctor.'

It was Heidi, although, for a moment I had forgotten her name. '. . . How are you? . . . and how is Helmut?' I asked.

'We are getting on just fine, thank you doctor. Helmut is feeling well also, I am pleased—and relieved to say. You know, doctor, he has completely changed his lifestyle. He still continues with his work, but at a much slower pace. His sole commitment is to getting well again. So now his days are organised around that commitment. He meditates three times every day, drinks many vegetable juices, keeps to a very strict anti-cancer diet and takes many herbal, mineral and vitamin supplements.'

'Is he still seeing the oncologist?' I asked.

'Well, actually, he isn't. You see, there is not much point. Apart from chemotherapy there was nothing else the oncologist could offer, and he certainly didn't offer any hope. We are so very pleased that he is feeling well and is still in his own way busy ... but as I said, not as busy as before. Helmut wouldn't be Helmut if he wasn't being creative.'

It was not long after my meeting with Heidi that Helmut presented in my surgery for a referral for a blood test. The results gave me a pleasant surprise. His liver function, indeed, his entire blood chemistry was virtually perfect. I suggested that a CT scan was timely. Helmut willingly agreed. Again, to my great surprise the results indicated no change; no spread. This was hardly how a cancer of his type would behave. I found the results remarkable.

Another six months passed. Helmut duly came to see me. We repeated the same routine. The results were the same as before. In the intervening months Helmut's name appeared in the local paper when his sculpture for the Cathedral was blessed by the Bishop. He certainly had a tremendous enthusiasm for living. One day Helmut phoned me to say that he and his wife were going back to visit relatives in Germany. They would be gone for three months as he also intended to make this a study tour. On his return he would come for his regular blood test and scan. I wished them both well, but could not help wondering how long his cancer could remain stable.

A few months later, in the midst of a particularly busy week I noticed Helmut's name in the appointments book. He had come complaining of abdominal pains. I asked him the routine questions and examined him. Nothing untoward.

'Here we go, the cancer has caught up with him,' I thought, without undue hesitation. He had a blood test and another abdominal scan. The blood test was completely normal, including his cancer tumour marker. The scan report showed only a slight trace of the cancer. The diagnosis—a lingering stomach virus from his overseas trip. I studied his case file again, carefully reading over his pathology reports. I discussed Helmut's case with my colleagues. A case of spontaneous remission was one that neither they nor I had encountered; medical journal material; remission without conventional treatment. I thought deeply about Helmut's passionate belief in his treatments, the strong emotional support that his wife had given him and his positive approach to life, so vividly demonstrated in his creativity. His case began my quest to know more about the mind–body connection and the power of the mind to heal. For the first time in my medical career I realised that statistics and pathology reports reveal only half the picture and that the person is as significant a variable as the disease.

Paul Kraus

The Dimensions of Faith

In some ways faith is a paradox. It is essentially a simple thing—a matter of complete trust; a strongly held belief, irrespective of whether or not logical proof exists. Yet, we are often unwilling to grasp a particular belief, or a strong hope. We seem unwilling to accept anything that is not tangible. The very simplicity of having a childlike faith is its greatest stumbling-block. We have a tendency to intellectualise everything. Late twentieth-century theologians have called our age one of 'unbelief.' We often confuse faith with wishful thinking, which means we are incapable of 'letting go and letting God', probably because our belief in God is weak.

Yet, even within a Biblical context, faith has a mysterious dimension. Anyone who has read the Book of Job will readily agree. Faith, like suffering, can never be fully understood in this life. In some ways, faith, like belief, is a gift from God. The wonderful thing is that it is a gift that anyone can humbly receive. Humility is a precondition of both belief and faith.

Faith is never a guarantee that healing will take place, although it is very frequently a precondition for healing. This is clearly illustrated in the healings which Jesus performed, which are recorded in the gospels, especially in the gospel of St Luke. What follows is a brief account of different kinds of faith which usually precede or accompany healing.

The focus of our faith should always be God and His wisdom. Throughout the Bible there are instances of the role which faith has played in the lives of individuals down through the ages. Perhaps the most comprehensive summary of faith is found in the Book of Hebrews: 'Now faith is the assurance of things hoped for, the conviction of things not seen ... By faith we understand that the world was created by the word of God, so that what is seen was made out of things which do not appear ...'. The writer goes on to chronicle a long list of examples of the faith of the patriarchs, such as Abraham and Moses. At the end of these historical examples of people of faith, the writer states: 'And all these, though well attested by their faith, did not receive what was promised, since God had foreseen something better for us' (Hebrews 11: 39).

This leads logically to the next aspect of faith, that God is faithful to His promises to hear and answer our prayers, *although not necessarily in the way we expect*. We must be prepared to realise that God's wisdom far surpasses ours and that healing will take place in the way He knows best.

Another aspect of faith is in His power. Only God can perform miracles. Nothing is impossible to God. Miracles were not confined to Biblical times. We need to have faith and trust that they are still capable of occurring. Likewise, we need to have faith in God's goodness. If we do so, we will see God's love shining through in every situation, even in the darkest tragedy.

Ultimately, the focus of our faith must always be in God, not in our own strength, or in our own faith. Francis MacNutt, who has had a remarkable healing ministry for over twenty years, wrote a book which has become a classic in its field. In *Healing*, he writes with deep spiritual wisdom about faith in relation to prayers for healing: 'Without discernment, which is a gift from God to know when to pray and when not to pray, we are bound to have some doubts when we pray—not doubts about God but about our own knowledge of God's will in a particular situation.' (*Healing*, Creation House, Florida, 1995, pp. 126–127)

Faith and Healing: Psalm 23

The Lord is my shepherd, I shall not want;
He makes me lie down in green pastures,
He leads me beside still waters;
He restores my soul.
He leads me in paths of righteousness for his name's sake.
Even though I walk through the valley of the shadow of death
I fear no evil;
for You are with me.
Your rod and Your staff they comfort me.
You prepare a table before me in the presence of my enemies;
You anoint my head with oil, my cup overflows.
Surely goodness and mercy shall follow me all the days of my
   life;
and I shall dwell in the house of the Lord for ever.

Faith and Hope

Faith gives substance to hope. Only faith can make the connection, the leap into the realms of the hoped for, the longed for, and make the way open for God who alone can bring it to pass.

Hope is the bridge over which faith walks hand-in-hand with God. And God who sees the end from the beginning, who calls things that are not as though they were, who speaks the word and it is so, sees a seed—and by perfect faith calls it a ripened ear of corn, or even a sheath ... or even again, a whole field full, ready for harvest.

Catherine Aldis
Used by permission of Wholeness *magazine, New Zealand*

Healing Is ...

HEALING IS filling your mind with God's love and releasing all guilt

HEALING IS turning towards God and away from disease and depression

HEALING IS joining your mind and will to God's mind and will

HEALING IS replacing fear with love, anger with peace, guilt with forgiveness

HEALING IS seeing yourself as forgiven and taking delight in it

HEALING IS inner peace which overflows the body

HEALING IS the same as forgiveness

HEALING IS thanking God for what He has already given you

HEALING IS correcting our vision of self, others and God

HEALING IS reconciliation between mind and spirit

HEALING IS being humble before God but being powerful in Him

HEALING IS freedom from past guilt and anxiety over the future

Author unknown

Tell All the World for Me

Faith is to believe what we do not see, and the reward of faith is to see what we believe.

St Augustine

Some fourteen years ago, I stood watching my university students file into the classroom for the opening session in my 'Theology of Faith' class. That was the first day I saw Tommy. He was combing his long flaxen hair, which hung six inches below his shoulders. I know it's what's in your head, not on it, that counts; but at that time I was unprepared for Tommy and wrote him off as strange—very strange.

Tommy turned out to be the atheist-in-residence in my course. He constantly objected to, or smirked at the possibility of an unconditionally loving God. We lived in relative peace for one semester, although at times he was a pain in the back pew. At the end of the course when he turned in his final exam, he asked in a slightly cynical tone, 'Do you ever think I'll find God?'

I decided on a little shock therapy. 'No!' I said emphatically.

'Oh,' he responded. 'I thought that was the product you were pushing.'

I let him get five steps from the door, then called out, 'Tommy! I don't think you'll ever find Him, but I am certain that He will find you!'

Tommy just shrugged and left. I felt slightly disappointed that he had missed my clever line.

Later I heard that Tom had graduated and I was duly grateful. Then came a sad report: Tom had terminal cancer. Before I could search him out, he came to me. When he walked into my office, his body was badly wasted. His long hair had fallen out because of chemotherapy. But his eyes were bright and his voice was firm for the first time in a long time.

'Tommy, I've thought about you often. I hear you are sick.' I blurted out.

'Oh yes, very sick. I have cancer. It's a matter of weeks.'

'Can you talk about it?'

'Sure, what would you like to know?'

'What's it like to be 24 and know you are dying?'

'Well, it could be worse!'

'Like what?'

'Well, like being 50 and having no values or ideals. Like being 50 and thinking that booze, seducing women and making money are the real biggies in life. But what I came to see you about is something you said to me on the last day of class. I asked if you ever thought I would find God and you said no, which surprised me. Then you said, "But He will find you". I thought about that a lot, even though my search was hardly intense at the time. But when the doctors removed a lump from my groin and told me it was malignant, I got serious about locating God. And when the malignancy spread to my vital organs, I really began banging against the doors of heaven. But nothing happened. Well, one day I woke up, and instead of throwing a few more futile appeals to a God who may or may not exist, I just quit. I decided I didn't care about God and the afterlife—or anything else for that matter.

'I decided to spend what time I had left doing something more profitable. I thought about you and something you had said in one of your lectures: "The essential sadness is to go through life without loving." But it would be equally sad to leave this world without telling those you love that you have loved them. So I began with the hardest one: my dad.

'He was reading when I approached him. "Dad, I would like to talk to you".

'"Well, talk," he replied. "I mean, it's really important, Dad." The newspaper came down three slow inches. "What is it?" he asked. "Dad, I love you, I just wanted you to know that."'

Tom smiled at me and said with obvious satisfaction, as though he felt a warm and secret joy flowing inside him, 'The newspaper fluttered to the floor. Then my father did two things I couldn't remember him doing before. He cried and he hugged me. And we talked all night even though he had to go to work the next day.

'It was easier with my mom and little brother. They cried with me, too, and we hugged each other and shared things we had been keeping secret for so many years. I was only sorry that we had waited so long. Here I was, in the shadow of death, and I was just beginning to open up to all the people I had actually been close to. Then one day I turned around and God was there. He didn't come to me when I pleaded with him. Apparently, God does things His own way at His own hour. The important thing is you were right. He found me even after I stopped looking for Him.'

'Tommy,' I gasped, 'I think you're saying something much more universal than you realise. You are saying that the surest way of finding God is not to make Him a private possession or an instant consolation in time of need, but rather by opening up to love.

'Tom, could I ask you a favour? Would you come to my "Theology of Faith" class and tell my students what you have just told me?'

Though we scheduled a date, he never made it. Of course, his life was not really ended by his death, it was only changed. He made the great step of faith into vision. He found a life far more beautiful than the eye of man has ever seen or the mind of man has ever imagined.

Before Tom died, we talked one last time. 'I'm not going to make it to your class,' he said.

'I know, Tom.'

'Will you tell them for me? Will you tell . . . the whole world for me?'

'I will, Tom. I'll tell them.'

John Powell

Reprinted with permission of Health Communications, Inc.,
Deerfield Beach, Florida, USA.

Hope and Joy

The close link between mind and body, as evidenced by the placebo effect, is vividly illustrated in the next two extracts from the best-selling book Peace, Love and Healing *by Bernie Siegel, an American surgeon. In the introduction Siegel writes: 'It is my feeling that no longer should medicine be only a mechanistic specialty that deals with the unexplained by calling it miraculous. Now is the time to reopen our study of the healing process and alter the way medicine approaches it, to turn our attention from disease and death to health and life.'*

The first of the two extracts gives an indication of the power and potential of hope to improve a person's quality of life and to aid in the healing process. The second extract is an interesting case study of Dr Siegel's which dramatically shows the potential of hope and joy to heal. It is one of those cases which Siegel cites in his introduction as 'miraculous' in the eyes of most doctors. These extracts are reproduced with the publisher's permission.

Anything that offers hope has the potential to heal, including thoughts, suggestions, symbols and placebos. Many still think that placebos may be fine for 'psychosomatic' problems but not for anyone with AIDS, cancer, multiple sclerosis or heart disease. It's interesting that this point of view has been with us for so long, despite innumerable studies showing that placebos can alleviate problems ranging, as psychologist Robert Ornstein and Dr David Sobel have tallied them, from 'post-operative wound pain; seasickness; headaches ... and other disorders of nervousness ... to high blood pressure; angina; depression; acne; asthma ... insomnia; arthritis ... lipoprotein levels and more.'

As Ornstein and Sobel put it, 'if such a treatment suddenly became available, we would believe that we had discovered a new wonder drug comparable to penicillin. Moreover, no system of the body appears immune to the effect.' ...

The more we learn about mind and body as a unity, the more difficult it becomes to consider them separately. What's in your mind is often quite literally, or 'anatomically,' what is in your body: peptide messenger molecules manufactured by the brain and the immune system are the link.

In January, 1983 John Florio, a seventy-eight-year-old landscape gardener was contemplating retirement. He developed abdominal pain and underwent a GI series, which showed an ulcer. He was treated for one month and re-X-rayed to see if the ulcer had healed. This time, however, it was larger and looked malignant. A biopsy revealed cancer of the stomach.

I first met John in late February when he was referred to my office for surgery. I suggested to him that we get him into the hospital right away since I was going on vacation, and I thought that with a rapidly advancing cancer he ought to have surgery immediately. He looked at me and said, 'You forgot something.' 'What did I forget?' I asked. 'It's Springtime. I'm a landscape gardener, and I want to make the world beautiful. That way if I survive, it's a gift. If I don't, I will have left a beautiful world.'

Two weeks after my vacation, he returned to the office, saying, 'The world is beautiful, I'm ready.' He looked incredibly well the night after his surgery, with no pain or discomfort. The pathology report revealed: 'Adenocarcinoma, poorly differentiated, invasive through gastric wall and into perigastric adipose tissue. Proximal margin involved by tumour, seven of sixteen lymph nodes positive for tumour.'

That simply meant he had a lot of cancer left in him after the operation. I explained to him that he ought to consider chemotherapy and X-ray therapy to deal with the residual cancer. 'You forgot something,' he said. 'What did I forget this time?' 'It's still Spring. I don't have time for all that.' He was totally at peace, healed rapidly and was out of the hospital well ahead of schedule.

Two weeks later he was back in my office, complaining that his stomach was upset, and I thought, 'Aha, it's the cancer again.' It turned out to be a virus, which I treated symptomatically, and he left my office.

In March 1987 I saw John's name in the chart rack. 'You must have the wrong chart.' I said to the nurse.

41

'No, that's the right chart,' she said.

'Then there must be two people with the same name.'

'No, no,' she insisted 'he's sitting in there.'

Then I showed her his pathology report to explain why I assumed she had made a mistake. If you think pathology reports predict the future for an individual, it wouldn't seem possible that I could be seeing John four years after his operation. But that's who I saw when I walked into my examining room.

I again feared that his visit would be related to cancer. Before I could ask him anything the first words out of his mouth were, 'Don't forget, this is only my second post-operative visit.' I think he wanted to make sure the insurance would cover it.

'But why are you here?' I asked.

'I have a question,' he said. 'I'd like to know what you can eat after a stomach operation.'

'Four years after—*anything!* But tell me, why are you here?'

'I have a hernia from lifting boulders in my landscape business.'

Since he refused to be admitted to the hospital, I repaired it under local anasthesia on an out-patient basis, and he was off and running again. If he rested at all, I'd be surprised, even though he promised to have two young men do his normal work the first few weeks after surgery.

John is one of those exceptional patients who seem to most clinicians to defy understanding. But I have learned that all these exceptional patients have stories to tell and lessons to teach. It's not just a matter of being lucky or having 'well-behaved' diseases (slow-growing tumours, 'spontaneous remissions' and so forth). What you have to understand is that there is a biology of the individual as well as a biology of the disease, each affecting the other. On the day of diagnosis we don't know either well enough to use a pathology report to predict the future.

It is now six years after his surgery, and John celebrated his eighty-third birthday recently. You have to wonder—what has happened to his cancer?

Bernie Siegel, MD

An Aura of Hope

This poem shows the vital importance of the doctor–patient relationship as a determinant in a patient's ability to recover from an illness. Statistics about a serious illness are one thing; recognition by the doctor of the uniqueness of each individual is another.

for Professor Avni Sali

Clinging to hope, sweet precious hope.
'False hope'—some claim so clinically.
I cannot abide—cannot cope
believing false hope exists. Cynically,
Science is their God;
the patient—a statistical curiosity.
Eminent in his field, specifically he denies
that cancer can't be cured. Optimistically
he avers that everyone can have a healing path—
thus denying all forms of negativity.
He welcomes questions—sympathetically,
carefully listening to my concerns.
Like Hygeia from ancient Greece,
he believes that natural laws assist in healing.
He encourages the mind's sealing
only positive, affirming thoughts
to activate, to gravitate, to stimulate
the physiology of hope.
A beacon of light—an empowering voice
of comfort in the wilderness of choice
and medical chance called oncology.
With him I know there's always a choice
to journey on a healing path in peace—
with Faith, Hope and Love that will not cease;
empowering me, inspiring me to persevere,
to leave alone the future and its fear.
He encourages me, convinces me
to laugh, to sing sweet melodies and see

43

miracles unfold each day.
Diet, meditate and pray,
always believing
that the best is yet to be.

Paul Kraus

The Physiology of Hope

Helen had just finished dressing. She sat down opposite Dr Harvey's desk . . . waited . . . and waited. His note-making seemed to go on unduly. As she watched him continue to write, ripples of anxiety began to disturb Helen's equilibrium. The only sound was the tap-tapping of his fingers on the keyboard of his computer. As the silence became further protracted, she felt the urge to speak. What on earth could he be writing about for so long? She felt totally well and had been so ever since her hysterectomy a year ago. At last he stopped typing.

'Is everything alright, doctor?' she asked, trying to sound unruffled.

'I think it probably is, especially in the light of your answers to my questions earlier, Mrs Douglas. I am just a tiny bit concerned about a suggestion of a lump I felt during the examination . . .'

Helen's heart rate accelerated rapidly . . . she felt an adrenalin rush as her mind went into full-alert mode. Dr Harvey looked at her, 'Please, Mrs Douglas . . . I'm not suggesting that anything's the matter. Rather, I think we should be careful and make sure that this slight lump I felt is nothing more than scar tissue from last year's surgery. I'd like you to have a routine blood test—in the course of which we'll test everything. If the results are all reasonably normal, then there's no need to come and see me for another twelve months. Otherwise, we'll discuss the matter further. In any case, I'll be writing to your doctor in the next day or two, letting him know what I have suggested. Would you like me to write a referral for the blood test, or would you prefer Dr Watson to write one for you?'

'Since I'm here, I may as well take it with me,' Helen said, trying to suppress her agitation. Intuitively, she felt that he wasn't telling her what he was really thinking. There was a slight reticence, almost reluctance to talk further about the possibilities of this lump he had felt. The word 'lump' had been enough to put her into a sweat.

Within the next two minutes Dr Harvey had filled in the

pathology request sheet. Helen watched him. She wondered what he was really thinking ... indeed, if he was thinking anything at all. After all, how many times had he followed this procedure? Unexpectedly ... quite irrationally, Helen felt animosity welling up. Why? He was only doing what was in her best interest. In her agitated state, she thought that his approach was too detached, too clinical. There was an aloofness about him that she suddenly found disconcerting. He played the role of gynaecologist with consummate polish. Usually, this did not bother her, but now, his manner lacked emotional support. Why didn't he go to greater lengths to reassure her that everything is alright ... that what he found was more or less routine?

Dr Harvey handed Helen the pathology referral. 'Dr Watson and I should have a copy of the results within a day or two of having the blood test. Pop along and see him and we'll take it from there. In the meantime, don't worry. As I said, it's as well to check these things out completely.'

'... And how did you go at the doctor's, darling?' asked David, when she walked in the door.

'Not too well at all. In fact, he's made me quite worried.'

'Why, what happened?' he asked, with the same awry look as he had just over a year ago when Helen broke the news of her impending hysterectomy.

'Well, I hope not. It's just that he thought he detected what he called "a suggestion of a lump" during his routine examination.'

'Not again?' he asked, with a hint of desperation.

'A lump ... yes, that's what I said ... a lump, although he didn't sound too alarmed ... wants me to have a blood test just to make sure everything is alright.'

David put his arms around his wife and gave her a hug and a long kiss. He was a big bear of a man with a warm, spontaneous smile and an ever-cheerful personality. He and Helen had been married for thirty-one years—a marriage which, unlike a number of their friends, had never faltered. He was fifty-seven; she fifty-four. Both their children had left home. Their son, Peter, was ordained as a minister in the Uniting Church at the beginning of the year and was appointed as assistant chaplain at a Church school in country New South Wales. He was to be married at the end of the year. Judy, their daughter, was expecting her first child within a month. The Douglas's had always been a closely knit family. Helen's excitement at the thought that she would soon be a grandmother was contagious. Each night mother and daughter would exchange the news of the day.

'Don't mention anything about your visit to Dr Harvey to Judy, will you, darling?'

'Of course not, David. Heavens, I wouldn't want to upset her. Besides, I just know deep down that the tests will be fine. I'm having the blood test to-morrow and seeing Alan Watson about them on Monday. Hopefully, if they're clear, I won't need to see Dr Harvey for twelve months.'

The sword of Damocles hovered over their heads for the next few days till Alan Watson, their GP, phoned.

'Helen, I'm just phoning to say that the blood test results are back. Would you be able to come and see me at 4 this afternoon?'

'Yes, I'll be there. Everything alright, I trust?'

'We'll talk about it this afternoon. Look forward to seeing you then.'

'Helen, I've had a chat with Dr Harvey about these results. He would like you to go and see him as soon as possible.'

Helen's heart began to pound. 'What do *you* think is the matter, Alan? Why am I anaemic again and why is the liver function abnormal?'

Alan Watson sighed deeply, looked at Helen's file, glanced again at the test results and looked directly in her frightened eyes, 'Look, Helen, you won't like me for saying this, but I honestly don't know. I could take a couple of educated guesses, but medicine is not about guesswork. It may well be nothing to worry about. Let's wait and see what Dr Harvey suggests. I think that at this stage, the most sensible way forward is to have these results investigated further.'

'Alan, let's not beat round the bush ... do you think it's cancer?'

'Well, of course there's a possibility that it might be. A couple of the results point in that direction ... but Helen ... remember,

47

that even if that were the case, there is a great deal that can be done. I realise that it must be very, very difficult, but try to keep this whole thing in perspective. Let's take this one step at a time. I know that Dr Harvey is an outstanding man. You couldn't possibly be in better hands.'

Dr Harvey ordered more tests. The ultrasound examination revealed 'a left pelvic mass consistent with ovarian origin'. Dr Harvey strongly suggested surgery to 'go in and have a look at the situation.'

'I suppose I don't have much choice, do I doctor?'

'Well, you certainly have a choice, Mrs Douglas. However, you are taking a great risk if you don't follow this up. If this lump is cancerous, we still have a chance to do something about it. At this stage we can still treat it. However, if you neglect things, then your condition could begin to deteriorate . . .'

Helen was booked in to have surgery in three weeks. A few days following the news of her surgery, to their great joy, she and David became proud grandparents—an event which cushioned the alarming news of her need for surgery. Helen went to stay with Judy to help her for the first week after she brought her beautiful healthy little son home. It was during that week Helen broke the news of her forthcoming surgery to her daughter.

'I didn't want to say anything to you before our darling little Michael was born,' Helen told her daughter on that first night, just after Michael had been bathed, fed and put into his cot. Before Judy had fully registered the news, Helen went on, 'I've had a number of tests done in the past three weeks. The results have given Dr Harvey cause for concern. One of them was an ultrasound which suggested I had a lump of what he called ovarian origin.'

Judy looked at her mother. The words she had just heard badly shook her composure. Her voice faltered, 'How have you been feeling? You look so well. In fact, when you came to see us in the hospital last week, I even commented to Mark that you almost look too young to be a grandmother.'

'I feel fine, really, I do. My appetite's good . . . apart from the occasional headache caused by the anxiety of these ongoing tests, I feel perfectly alright. As a matter of fact, Dr Harvey thinks there may be some connection between my last operation and the current problems. By the way, I told Alan Watson last week the wonderful news about Michael's safe arrival. He was thrilled and asked to be remembered to you. I told him there are far too many exciting things going on in my life at the moment to be worried about illness of any kind. He empathised with my feelings.'

The week Helen spent with Judy and her young family was an invigorating tonic. When David came to pick her up, he was pleased to see how well Helen looked. He was so happy for her. Being together with his family took his mind off the worry of Helen's impending hospitalisation. As they drove home, their conversation centred upon Judy and Mark's new addition to the family and on Peter's forthcoming marriage which was less than three months away.

Dr Harvey's reputation as a gynaecological oncologist was very high. It was a reputation based on his skills as a clinician and researcher. He was regularly overseas presenting papers at international conferences. Doctors from around Australia liaised with him about difficult cases. Not infrequently he operated on patients from great distances. Helen and David realised that she was in the best available medical care. Helen never doubted Dr Harvey's knowledge or skills. It was something about his manner— a certain haughtiness, that made her uncomfortable with him. She felt that he was too much of a medical scientist. As such, he forgot the vital fact that medicine was as much an art as it was a science. She felt that, in spite of his high reputation, he was not a good listener; that he concentrated exclusively on the disease and ignored her as a person. Maybe, it was just that there was a slight clash of personalities. Maybe?

David was sitting anxiously in the waiting room on the floor directly under the operating suite. The television fastened to the wall hadn't bothered him for a while, but as the minutes turned into an hour, then almost two, it had become an irritant, with its mindless chattering noise. He had brought a book to read—one of Helen's books on healing, but his mind was far too restless to read.

Dr Harvey walked into the room in a double-breasted suit and starched collar. He came straight across to David, 'Mr Douglas ... pleased to meet you. Do come this way.' They shook hands and the doctor opened a door adjacent to where they were standing. They walked in and sat down on two comfortably padded chairs. Dr Harvey closed the door behind them.

'I'm sure you will be pleased to know that Mrs Douglas came through the surgery very well. She'll be in recovery for a little while longer, but you should be able to go up to the ward and see her within the next forty-five minutes or so. I'm afraid the news is not so good. I found a large tumour in the left and central pelvis, extensively involving the small and large bowel. She had a large number of lesions throughout the pelvic and abdominal cavities. I've taken samples to have biopsied. Until we get back the pathology results, I'm not prepared to say what type of cancer we're looking at, but, unfortunately, Mr Douglas, there's no doubt at all that it is cancer.'

David stared blankly at the doctor. He was stunned ... speechless. The words he had just heard had scrambled his mind. He desperately tried to find an appropriate response. None was forthcoming. The two men sat for a few moments in an awful silence, which was broken as Dr Harvey gave a brief sigh. His demeanour brightened. He went on, 'Looking on the brighter side, Mr Douglas ... a lot depends on what the pathologists come up with ... and we must remember that there is a great deal that can be done in the way of treatment ...'

'How long till the pathology results come back, doctor?'

'They should be back in a week's time, although they could take a little longer. Be absolutely assured that I'll let you know immediately when we have any news.'

'What's the treatment involve, doctor?'

'Well, of course, that depends on what type of cancer it is. However, it would almost certainly be chemotherapy. We'll have to wait for a week or so before we know what the next step is to be.'

The ensuing week brought Helen and David closer than they had ever been. Helen's spirit was uplifted by David's loving support.

'We'll beat this, darling ... you have so much to live for ... you're going to see Peter married shortly ... we're going to be there when he's awarded his doctorate in a couple of years' time ... together we're going to see his family grow ... together we're going to watch little Michael growing up ... we've so much living to enjoy together ... God-willing. We've survived other hurdles over the past thirty-one years. We're going to survive this.'

As he embraced her, she felt the warmth of his love energise her. His smile drove away her fear. Peter came to see his mother every night. Judy and her husband came with little Michael to the hospital to see their mother. Get-well cards and messages of assurance and hope arrived. Friends came to see Helen as soon as she was well enough. Their local minister came to visit. He firmly held her hand as he prayed for her. The tears streamed down her cheeks when he had finished praying. She felt as though she was enfolded by love on every side.

The pathology report came back and described the biopsies as 'malignant tumour with moderate variation in cell size and shape ... a poorly differentiated carcinoma, possibly of ovarian origin'. This was hardly the news they had hoped for. Dr Harvey decided on further surgery in the short term as the way forward.

Three weeks later Helen was back in the operating theatre. This time the surgeon removed the mass and attached portions of small and large bowel. She was left with a colostomy and obvious tumour still in her abdomen.

Again David endured the purgatory of the wait while his wife underwent extensive surgery. This time the prognosis was somewhat bleaker. 'Unfortunately, Mr Douglas, your wife's cancer is quite aggressive. It has already invaded a large area.'

'What is the outlook, doctor?'

'Not too good, I'm afraid. I discovered that she has developed widespread metastatic throughout the abdominal cavity.'

'How much time do you feel that she has left, doctor?'

'Hard to say, really. I've seen similar cases where patients have outlived their expected prognosis far longer than was expected. However, given what I've just seen, I think we would be expecting months, rather than years. I'm going to recommend to Dr Jones, the oncologist, that she commence chemotherapy as soon as possible. The colostomy should be able to removed fairly soon, I hope.'

Helen took the news remarkably well. Indeed, the hospital staff were amazed at her plucky spirits and were touched at David's deep devotion to his wife. Each day he arrived in Helen's ward with a large bag which he emptied with the excitement of a child on Christmas Day. He was never dry-eyed when he left. Helen's positive outlook was inspirational to the two other patients in her ward, to the extent that they formed a close bond with her and when it was time for her to go home the three ladies promised each other to keep in touch.

A fortnight later Helen and David found themselves in Dr Jones's rooms. They sat anxiously as the oncologist reviewed her scans, her ultrasounds and quickly read her file. He then proceeded to examine her, at the end of which Helen and David sat waiting to hear what treatment protocol he would recommend. Dr Jones gave his patient a sympathetic look, 'As your surgeon has probably indicated, Mrs Douglas, your condition is rather serious.' Dr Jones was economical with his words, 'I would recommend that we start you on a course of chemotherapy without delay. Hopefully, if your cancer responds, we should be able to close the colostomy after the first treatment finishes.'

'And when would that likely to be?' asked Helen.

'In about four to six months.'

'What is the success rate with this type of chemotherapy, doctor?'

'Somewhere in the order of 50%. Perhaps slightly higher.'

'I suppose this treatment comes with nasty side-effects ... nausea, loss of appetite, hair loss and so on?'

'Yes, I'm afraid it does, Mrs Douglas ... although, of course, some people are affected much less than others ... I strongly recommend you commence this treatment without too much delay, Mrs. Douglas . . . the longer the delay, the less chance we have of a successful outcome.'

Without hesitating, Helen short-circuited the conversation, 'I'm not prepared to have chemotherapy, doctor. I intuitively know that it's not the right treatment for me.' She spoke forthrightly.

'Well, needless to say, the decision is entirely up to you, Mrs Douglas, but I believe your best chance lies with what I have just recommended.'

'I knew before I came to see you that chemotherapy was the only treatment for my condition, but I fervently believe it is not the right way to go.'

'I'm not sure that there is any other way to go, Mrs Douglas,' Dr Jones replied. There was a lengthy pause.

'With God's help, we'll win this battle. I believe that miracles are wrought by prayer,' Helen replied confidently.

'I wish you well, Mrs Douglas. Should you change your mind, I would be pleased to see you at any time.'

A couple of days before her consultation with Dr Jones, Helen and David had been to the healing service at the cathedral. She had the laying on of hands and had been anointed with oil. It was a transcendental experience—the like of which she had never previously encountered. She felt a deep warmth radiate throughout her body as that ceremony proceeded. In the fleeting, precious moments of the hymns and prayers she felt completely uplifted, completely at peace. As she meditated and prayed later that night, Helen had heard a reassuring voice emerge from that silence whispering to her that all will be well.

Very early the next morning Helen wrote a long letter to her elderly mother, with whom she had had no dealings for many years. It was a letter of reconciliation and forgiveness; it was also a letter which brought a great sense of release. A burden she had been carrying for so long had suddenly been lifted.

During her first spell in hospital a friend brought Helen a book on how to cope with cancer. She eagerly read it—and read it again, carefully annotating it, with a view to putting its advice into practice. It was a book which set out all the approaches to treating this disease, both conventional and complementary. It was almost like a handbook on improving one's quality of life.

Helen radically changed her diet to a high-fibre, low-fat, low-sugar vegetarian regime which incorporated an abundance of vegetable juices each day. She began taking anti-oxidant vitamins and minerals, special amino acids and other supplements. She also started gentle exercises each day and she incorporated visualisation of tumour shrinkage into her daily meditation. She went to the city each week for the healing service in the cathedral. She had incorporated these things into her life when she and David visited the oncologist soon after her discharge from hospital. Above all, Helen was surrounded by the love of her family. Her anticipation of Peter's forthcoming marriage energised her with hope.

Shortly after her visit to the oncologist, she returned to her GP's surgery.

'And how are you feeling, Helen? . . . How did go with your visit to Dr Jones? I haven't heard from him yet. It usually takes a little while . . .'

'I'm feeling well, thanks, Alan . . . In fact, I seem to be feeling stronger each day, I really do.'

'Well, I must say you are looking a whole lot better than you did last time I saw you just before leaving hospital a fortnight ago.'

Helen discussed her visit to the oncologist with Alan Watson. At first Alan was a little alarmed by her refusal to submit to the chemotherapy treatment.

'But that's all he could offer me . . . a treatment with only a 50% success rate and one which would be detrimental to my quality of life—a highly toxic and lengthy treatment which would severely suppress my already fragile immune system. I know in my heart of hearts that such a treatment would kill me. Equally, I know that with God's help, I'll win this battle . . .' She told Alan Watson exactly what regime she was pursuing, 'David actually typed out my daily plan . . . here, I'll leave a copy with you.'

Alan Watson cast his eye down the page which listed all her supplements, juices and the details of her diet. The combination of Alan's holistic approach to medicine and Helen's poor prognosis predisposed him to being sympathetic and supportive of the path Helen had chosen to take. He knew what an iron-willed lady she was. Not exactly stubborn—rather resolute. He was also aware of her strong religious faith, the emotional support she had from her family and her positive outlook on life. 'I guess that now it's a case of closely monitoring your condition, Helen. If the need arose, I know that Dr Jones would be happy to see you. In the meantime, come and see me on a regular basis. I'll arrange that you have another blood test shortly.'

Four weeks passed quickly. Helen's sole preoccupation was in getting well. She kept strictly to her daily routine, which included meditation, prayer, yoga, juicing and cooking.

The results of the forthcoming blood test surprised, indeed astonished, Alan Watson. She was no longer anaemic and her liver function had returned to almost normal. Each visit brought an improvement in her condition.

A month further on and Helen went back to see her surgeon. 'Doctor, this colostomy is a dreadful burden. You must remove it . . . you really must. It's interfering with my recovery.'

'Mrs Douglas, I do not want to operate to remove it until you have chemotherapy treatment. You are very unwise to do anything else with your diagnosis.'

'Doctor, I don't want to give the impression that I am behaving like a stubborn mule, but I can tell you that I am feeling much better. My weight has returned to normal, I have a good appetite and I know this wretched thing is regressing.'

The doctor looked at Helen sympathetically. He could see that she was holding back the tears.

'Come back and see me in a month's time and I'll make a decision then. I feel that it is premature to contemplate removing it now. Even in a month, it is too early, but if your condition improves dramatically, then there's a strong chance I could do it for you.'

Circumstance dictated that the month stretched into three.

Yet again, David sat anxiously in the waiting room adjacent to the theatre suites. The length of the operation alarmed him. It was nearly an hour and a half after the surgeon said he would be down, that he finally appeared.

'The adhesions I encountered in the peritoneal cavity did not look good at all. I saw not dozens, but hundreds of three to nine millimetre peritoneal tumours. They appeared exactly as I had seen them in the previous surgery.'

The colour drained from David's face. 'But, she is getting on so well, doctor . . . she is feeling so well . . . if she is feeling as well as she does, then how is it possible that there is so much residual cancer?'

'I'll be able to answer your question when we get the biopsy result back from the pathologist, Mr Douglas. I have taken several tumours from various locations to be biopsied.'

Another agonising wait followed, although this time Helen's amazing recovery from the surgery ameliorated David's anxiety. She was bright and full of optimism.

At the prearranged time, David phoned the surgeon.

'Well, Mr Douglas, your wife is a very interesting lady, a very interesting lady indeed. The pathology results arrived back this morning. Let me read some of it for you. ". . . inflammatory tissue with moderate cell variation and *no malignant characteristics*" . . .'.

Helen shed tears of joy at Peter's wedding which took place just prior to Christmas. The New Year brought new hopes, new dreams and new plans. Helen continued her dietary regime, her daily meditation and prayer, and found a peace of mind she had never experienced before her diagnosis. She made such a concerted effort to ensure that her body was hostile to cancer.

In March her quarterly scan was due. Following her test she took the large envelope with the results to Alan Watson. He opened the package, stared at the report, whose hallmark was its brevity, stood up, walked around and gave his patient a warm embrace, 'Helen, this is absolutely wonderful . . . marvellous . . . congratulations! Your cancer's gone! It seems as though you're in remission! This is truly incredible.'

'Oh, don't congratulate me—please don't.'

'Yes, I most certainly do—with the huge effort you've made to get well!'

'All those months ago, when I refused the chemotherapy, I told Dr Jones that with God's help, I would win this battle— and I happened to do just that. At the same time time I was very conscious that if He wanted me in Heaven, then I was ready to go. Now, I know that He still has plans for me down here . . . there are things yet to be done . . . people whom maybe I can help.'

The report showed no residual peritoneal tumours. Helen's oncologist and surgeon were dumbfounded. They agreed that in this case there was no question of a mis-diagnosis. This was spontaneous remission, without a doubt.

Helen joined the Carer's group at the Cathedral Healing Ministry. She became a source of inspiration and hope to others. She spoke to others about the ways in which cancer had actually brought blessings into her life, like persuading her to live in the present and to leave the past behind, to be thankful for each day and to recognise the miraculous in the ordinary.

Paul Kraus

The Prognosis

Although a very personal piece of writing, this poem was written as an encouragement to those given a poor prognosis. The shock of receiving bad news can be profound but it is important to remember that the information doctors give their patients is based on statistics relating to a particular disease. No consideration is given to the fact that each case is unique and that many variables exist. These variables, such as the will to live, having support, having positive emotions such as peace, love and joy, adopting a radical dietary change and meditating can assist a person's ability to heal.

Like a judge entering the court
with a nurse as his sergeant-at-arms
my surgeon came to pass sentence.
I lay there, impotent,
like the prisoner in the dock.
He spoke in a detached, clinical way
of the evidence he'd seen
with the clarity of a laparoscopic lens;
of exhibits sent for pathological examination.
His explanation grated in the prisoner's ear—
curt—complete with injected fear.

Then with furrowed brow he paused.
With due deliberation, began his summing up:
(phrases carefully chosen from his standard repertoire)
'I'm sorry, very sorry,' he sighed,
'but in your case there's nothing we can do . . .'
The prisoner hung on every word—
quickly drained of hope.

'It's too widespread to stop it now . . .'
The prisoner asked, 'What clemency could I expect?'
His reply burnt like a searing iron:
'A few months, six at best . . . I'm sorry,'
was all he was prepared to say.

Even the wise judge (human as he was)
forgot the potential of appellant voices
to change the course of his decree—
voices which refused
to heed the verdict handed down;
felicitous healing voices—
of Hope, of Peace, of Love.

These voices, like angelic heralds came
to remit the fear,
to overturn the judge's non-parole
and to set the prisoner free.

Paul Kraus

Winter Sunset

No yesterdays
or tomorrows
—snapshot
of eternity.
Magical ambience,
mysterious twilight,
silver bank
of cumulus clouds
towering
like giant harlequins
filling the sky.
Halcyon mauve
calms inky sea.
What mighty
Hand wrought
this harmony?

Epilogue
to the day
—snapshot
of eternity.

Paul Kraus

LOVE

The Healing Power of Love

In a very real sense love, kindness and compassion heal. This sounds almost trite, but it is absolutely true. In all kinds of ways love does actually enhance the healing process. 'Healing' refers to attaining peace of mind, having freedom from fear and anxiety and experiencing unconditional love. The word 'healing' is not synonymous with 'cure'. Healing is certainly not restricted to a physical cure, which might or might not eventuate. Love and healing are always possible, irrespective of whether or not a cure takes place. On this side of the grave, we can never hope to understand the mystery of why some people recover, while others do not.

The road to healing has many different paths, according to our personality type, or our philosophy of life, but love is a fundamental attribute which transcends these variables. Love, like faith, means different things to different people, but whatever its meaning for an individual, most would agree that love has a spiritual dimension.

The poems, the short story and the writings in this section vividly illustrate the power of love to heal. Perhaps the most potent way that love heals is that it helps to release our fear. Fear, like anger, resentment and bitterness actually blocks a person's ability to heal, whereas love enhances the capacity of the body to heal itself.

Some of the following writings are specifically drawn from a person's religious experience, where that person felt the nearness of God at a critical point in their lives. Other writings in this section are more general and are included to illustrate the fact that we as human beings are all endowed with a spiritual dimension.

Faith and love are first cousins, so this section has a strong similarity with the writings on faith. The two are intertwined, with hope being closely related to both. If we are not capable of giving and receiving love, then something is missing from our lives and we become alienated from ourselves and others and are in need of healing.

Loving Others: Opening Your Heart

If I can stop one heart from breaking,
I shall not live in vain;
If I can ease one life the aching,
or cool one pain,
or help one fainting robin
Unto his nest again,
I shall not live in vain.

Emily Dickinson

If You Want to Be Happy

If you want to be happy for an hour
    take a nap.
If you want to be happy for a day
    go fishing.
If you want to be happy for a month
    get married.
If you want to be happy for a year
    inherit a fortune.
But if you want to be happy for a lifetime
    do something good for someone else.

Workshop Participant (Anonymous)

Extracts from Living, Loving and Healing
by Bernie Siegel, MD
Aquarian/Thorsons, New York, 1993.
Used with permission.

The Beautiful Colour of Love

What colour is God,
Asked the child with skin so fair
Is he white like me,
Does he have light hair

Is God dark like me,
Asked the child with skin of golden hue
Has he hair that's dark and curly,
Are his eyes black or blue

I think God is red like me,
The Indian boy is heard to say
He wears a crown of feathers,
And turns our nights to day

Each one of us knows that God is there,
In all the colours above
But be sure of this, the one colour he is,
Is the beautiful colour of love

So when your soul goes to Heaven,
When your life comes to its end
He will be waiting, and his hand to you
Will he extend.

There will be no colours in heaven,
Everyone will be the same.
You will only be judged by your earthly deeds,
Not your colour or your name

So when your time comes,
And you see God in his heaven above,
Then you will see the only colour that counts,
The beautiful colour of love.

Arnold (Sparky) Watts. Reproduced with permission.
Health Communications, Inc. 3201 S.W. 15th Street
Deerfield Beach, Fl 33442–8190

Love—A Biblical Perspective

So we know and believe the love God has for us. God is love, and he who abides in love abides in God, and God abides in him ... there is no fear in love, but perfect love casts out fear. For fear has to do with punishment, and he who fears is not perfected in love. We love because God first loved us. If anyone says, 'I love God,' and hates his brother, he is a liar; for he who does not love his brother whom he has seen, cannot love God, whom he has not seen. And this commandment we have from him, that he who loves God should love his brother also.

1 John 4: 16–21

If I speak in the tongues of men and of angels, but have not love, I am a noisy gong or a clanging cymbal. And if I have prophetic powers, and understand all mysteries and all knowledge, and if I have all faith, so as to remove all mountains, but have not love, I am nothing. If I give away all that I have, and if I deliver my body to be burned, but have not love, I gain nothing.

Love is patient and kind; love is not jealous or boastful; it is not arrogant or rude. Love does not insist on its own way; it is not irritable or resentful; it does not rejoice at wrong, but rejoices in the right. Love bears all things, believes all things, hopes all things, endures all things.

Love never ends; as for prophecy, it will pass away; as for tongues, they will cease; as for knowledge, it will pass away. For our knowledge is imperfect and our prophecy is imperfect; but when the perfect comes, the imperfect will pass away. When I was a child I spoke like a child, I thought like a child, I reasoned like a child; when I became a man, I gave up childish ways. For now we see in a mirror dimly, but then face to face. Now I know in part; then I shall understand fully, even as I have been fully understood.

So faith, hope, love abide, these three; but the greatest of these is love.

1 Corinthians 13: 1–13

Being Open to Love

In order to love who you are,
I must know who you are.
Otherwise I can only love
What I want you to be.
That's unfair to you; selfish of me,
And breeds disappointment.
Self revelation is essential to being loved
For what you are.
It demands trust, but it offers
The possibility of true love.
Not to reveal yourself to another,
Is never to believe
The real you is worth loving.

Gail Whiting in The Open Hand *magazine.*
Reproduced with permission of Wholeness *magazine,*
New Zealand.

Sonnet

The following poem, written many centuries ago by the greatest playwright in the English language, beautifully and simply captures the eternal nature of true love. Whilst it might seem slightly out of place in this anthology of writings on healing, it is included because the life-affirming truths it captures about love do not date. The truths it enshrines about the meaning of love are profound.

Let me not to the marriage of true minds
Admit impediments. Love is not love
Which alters when it alteration finds,
Or bends with the remover to remove:
O no! it is an ever fixed mark,
That looks on tempests and is never shaken;
It is the star to every wandering bark,
Whose worth unknown, although his height be taken.
Love's not Time's fool, though rosy lips and cheeks
Within his bending sickle's compass come;
Love alters not with his brief hours and weeks,
But bears it out even to the edge of doom:
If this be error and upon me proved,
I never writ, nor no man ever loved.

William Shakespeare

The Healing Within

In wisdom, Providence allowed this illness
to open wide the window of my heart—wide
enough that Love might come into the stillness.
Like a butterfly, Love landed by my side.
Imperceptibly, as if in a chrysalis state,
I saw its colours beautiful and clear:
blue, green, yellow and even slate.
Love bade me let go of all my fear.

Love suggested surrendering the past;
to see this as a sacrament of hope and healing.
Happiness, like a tiny lotus flower, came at last.
Wistful, first, then quite wonderful, this feeling,
this surging tide, this energy wherein the Kingdom dwells.

Paul Kraus

There Are Two Loves Only

We are made by love and for love. On earth we learn to love. At death we shall take our examinations on love. If we have trained ourselves well enough, we shall go and live eternally in Love. Now here below every time we love ourselves (selfishness) we fail a little in carrying out God's plans for us and for the world. There are but two loves, love of ourselves and love of God and of others.

To live is to choose between these two loves.

There are two loves only, Lord,
Love of myself and love of you and of others,
And each time that I love myself, it's a little less love for you
    and for others,
It's a draining away of love, it's a loss of love,
For love is made to leave self and fly towards others.
Each time it's diverted to myself, it withers, rots and dies.
Love of self, Lord, is a poison that I absorb each day;
Love of self chooses the best part and keeps the best place;
Love of self indulges my senses and supplies them from the
    table of others;
Love of self speaks about myself and makes me deaf to the
    words of others;
Love of self chooses, and forces that choice on a friend;
Love of self puts on a false front, it wants me to shine,
    overshadowing others;
Love of self is self-pitying and overlooks the suffering of
    others;
Love of self thinks me virtuous, it calls me a good man;
Love of self induces me to earn money, to spend it for my
    pleasure, to save it for my future;
Love of self advises me to give to the poor in order to ease my
    conscience and live in peace ...
Love of self is a stolen love,
It was destined for others, they needed it to live, to thrive,
    and I have diverted it.

So the love of self creates human suffering . . .
Help me to love, Lord,
not to waste my powers of love,
to love myself less and less in order to love others more and
    more,
That around me, no one should suffer or die because I have
    stolen the love they needed to live . . .

Michel Quoist, Prayers of Life
Gill & Macmillan, Dublin, 1969, pp. 79–80.
Reproduced with permission of the publisher.

Unconditional Love

Many people, especially cancer patients, grow up believing there is some terrible flaw at the centre of their being, a defect they must hide if they are to have any chance for love. Feeling unlovable and condemned to loneliness if their true selves become known, such individuals set up defences against sharing their innermost feelings with anyone. They feel their ability to love shrivelling up, which leads to further despair.

Dostoevsky expressed the feeling when he wrote, 'I am convinced that the only Hell which exists is the inability to love'. Because such people feel a profound emptiness inside, they come to see all relationships and transactions in terms of getting something to fill the vaguely understood void within. They give love only on condition that they get something for it, whether comfort, security, praise, or a similar love. This 'if' love is exhausting and prevents you from expressing your authentic self. It leads to an even deeper sense of emptiness, which keeps the vicious circle going.

I feel that all disease is ultimately related to a lack of love, or to love that is only conditional, for the exhaustion and depression of the immune system thus created leads to physical vulnerability. I also feel that healing is related to the ability to give and accept unconditional love . . .

When I can get people to accept themselves as whole individuals, lovable as they are, they become able to give from an inner strength. They find that unconditional love does not subtract from some limited emotional storehouse. Instead it multiplies itself. It feels good to give, it makes the recipient feel good, and sooner or later it returns . . . One of the immediate rewards is a 'live' message to the body. I am convinced that unconditional love is the most powerful known stimulant of the immune system. If I told patients to raise their blood levels of immune globulins or killer T cells, no one would know how. But if I can teach them to love themselves and others fully, the same changes happen automatically. The truth is: love heals . . . As the mediaeval German mystic Meister Eckhart wrote:

The bodily food we take is changed into us, but the spiritual food we receive changes us into itself; therefore divine love is not taken into us, for that would make two things. But divine love takes us into itself, and we are one with it.

From Love, Medicine and Miracles *by Bernie Siegel, MD*
Arrow Books, London, 1991.
Used with permission.

My Son's Graduation

for David

Unsuspectingly, like a thunderclap,
the recognition of his face in the crowd
shakes my emotions—deeply . . .
almost uncontrollably.

True, the doctor said I wouldn't live
to see this day, but kind Providence
pledged to gently lead me here.
Beyond this poignant reality
lies something more.

This crown of his recalls,
quite strangely,
—apocalyptically,
memories long lost
in the hidden corridors
of my mind.

His name is called.
He's run the race;
through God's good grace
attained his prize.
We shake each other's hand . . . I brace
myself . . . I rise
for appropriate words—
for meaningful, lasting words
which might echo down the length of time.

Unexpectedly, words fail
to come. Beyond the pain
they struggle, then sail
into oblivion.
Can he read my mind?
Feel my remorse,
my tender thoughts

and deep regrets ...

Of times we never shared ...
Of words we seldom spoke ...
Of smiles too rarely seen ...
Of laughter not enjoyed ...

His eyes sparkle, his smile
speaks joyfully and thankfully
that I am here to see what he has done:
for what he's strived
and has achieved,
for the healing that's begun.

Paul Kraus

Healing Partnerships

This story invites the reader to consider the way love heals at both an emotional and physical level. The 'healing partnerships' operate on different levels to produce hope in each of the characters. They all face difficulties, but through their love and support for each other they are able to confront, and finally overcome, the formidable problems each of them face.

The talk of mergers was no longer rumour but a fast approaching fact. John was a youthful fifty-two-year-old professional accountant. His last twenty years had been spent in the service of The Company. The heavy demands of the corporate world had compensations. For years the word 'security' was spelt in upper case. At that time John had a growing family, mortgage and the usual financial commitments of middle age. Twenty years' loyal service had ensured that those financial commitments were met and that the family could enjoy the usual trappings of middle-class suburbia: two cars in the garage, air-conditioned house and swimming pool.

The Company had been remarkably resilient to the ebb and flow of the economic tide in the past two decades. Of course there had been mergers, restructuring, with minor casualties, but nothing too dramatic. In recent times all that changed. The economic downturn rendered security an anachronism. Fortunately, both the children had left home and were independent. Peter was twenty-five and an officer cadet in the Air Force; Hannah twenty-three and working as a librarian in Canberra. John's wife Mary had for many years worked as a part-time teacher-librarian at the local primary school. Stability had been a hallmark of the Edwards family. Family landmarks and rituals were duly observed and recorded in the numerous framed photos sitting on the lounge-room sideboard.

John's familiar world—the world he had for so long taken for granted—fell apart. It was like a little death. Routine and stability were parts of the same equation. The effect was traumatic. Redundancy belonged to other sections of the company, not his. Had he been naive and misread the pace of rationalisation? Had the downturn in the market caught him by surprise? Who knew? What did it matter now?

The fact remained that the shock was profound. Half-expecting the end was one thing, but when it came, it was very hard to take: a kind of grieving, as it were. Not that the stages were clear-cut but they were nevertheless present: disbelief, denial, anger, sorrow; finally, acceptance. John and Mary had married twenty-seven years earlier. They met at university. It was love at first sight. Their marriage had never faltered. Mary was the more outgoing of the two, always cheerful. She was both practical and pragmatic. She accepted the news of John's redundancy without drama. They had mutually solved many crises. This one was not insuperable. John had a number of options, although he worried about his age. Over fifty and no-one wants to know you, irrespective of the quality of your CV. Nevertheless, there were numerous contacts to be followed up and his optimism was high.

John's actual redundancy coincided with the school holidays, which enabled them to go away together. They decided to pack their bags, forget about everything for ten days and take off to Noosa. They rented a comfortable little holiday flat along the river at Noosaville—a little piece of paradise.

Those ten days were like a second honeymoon. They rented a car, did numerous short trips around the Sunshine Coast and enjoyed the balmy late winter weather. The holiday was therapeutic. It strengthened John's hope and resolve of finding another job and it cushioned the shock with which John was still coming to terms. During their time away John drew up a strategy, a plan for finding a new job.

Within a fortnight of their return John had sent off seven applications. He was meticulous in ensuring that his applications met every requirement of the advertised positions. By the third week back his daily routine faltered. Watching for the mail and expectantly listening for the phone started to take a toll on his nerves. By the fifth week his score in the game of job-hunting had been three interviews but no actual job offers. Not a bad score for such a relatively short space of time. He had spent much time, effort and not an inconsiderable sum sending off applications. John had discovered that in his situation the old saying: 'No news is good news' did not apply. Mary measured John's moods by the time of the week. Each Monday morning started optimistically as he busied himself applying for positions from the Saturday paper. As the week wore on and the phone remained silent and the letterbox empty, his mood spiralled downwards. He had performed well in the interviews and was puzzled that none so far had been successful. Meaning and purpose had suddenly eclipsed security in John's quest for stability and self-esteem.

Then, quite unexpectedly, John's mind-set changed. As he picked up a mid-week paper from the newsagent, a copy of the 'Businesses for Sale' caught his eye. Impulsively, he picked it up and bought it. The idea of having his own business had crossed his mind—merely a passing thought.

'And how was your day? Any news?' Mary asked, as she put her things down in the kitchen and put the kettle on.

'Not a thing. I can't make out what's going on. Probably the moment they see my age, my application is consigned to the rejection pile.' The increasing sense of frustration was evident. John's growing negativity, cynicism and depression—the first cousins of anger and bitterness—were starting to worry Mary. 'Oh, I guess there was one interesting thing—at least, potentially interesting ...'

'What's that?' she asked expectantly, pleased at the way his spirit momentarily lifted.

'Well, I'm glad you're sitting down ... this might sound slightly crazy, Mary ... I know it would involve an enormous lifestyle change for us both, but ... something about it gave me a mild adrenalin rush ...'

'Well ... for goodness sake, what is it?' she asked impatiently.

John picked up the 'Businesses for Sale' he had bought. 'Look at this ...' He handed the magazine to her.

' "Health Food Shop For Sale ... Very solid business ... excellent trading figures, showing steady growth over the

78

past four years . . . ideal lifestyle . . . no competition . . . pleasant large country town . . . yet only two hours from the city . . . healthy climate . . . excellent amenities . . . this is an outstanding business opportunity in a growing industry . . . genuine enquiries only . . ." Mm . . . it's a thought . . . we would work well together . . . Ever since Hannah left, I've thought I could do with a change . . . I see what you mean, John. Why don't you follow this up?'

John's focus suddenly changed. The two rejection letters that came in the mail over the next few days lost their sting. The mere fact that Mary let him pursue this line of enquiry, indeed, encouraged him to investigate this possibility, buoyed his optimism. The owner faxed through the details—ten pages no less. John plunged into his detective work with thoroughness and vigour. The results looked promising. The current owners were delightful people—open and friendly. They had an enviable business record. They had combined integrity and honesty with a deep commitment to customer service and an excellent knowledge of natural remedies and wholefood nutrition. This had been the formula of their success.

'What did you know about this industry when you bought the business?' John asked the current owner.

'Very little, but I changed that situation very quickly.'

John was aware that success in small business depended on many variables and intangibles. He and Mary drove to Brighton on the weekend, met the owners and liked what they saw. What had been almost a flight of fancy a few days earlier, now suddenly loomed as an exciting possibility. John visited other health food shops, phoned some of the suppliers and even spoke to a naturopath acquaintance about the idea. The vibes were positive. John analysed the logistics of translating this idea into reality. He worked through various possibilities and carefully analysed the trading figures. Two more trips to Brighton followed in fairly quick succession. John and Mary decided to rent a house there for twelve months while they rented their own.

Negotiations with the current owners proceeded quickly. Two months later John and Mary Edwards formed a business partnership and began their new life. Their second journey—an adventurous mid-life change—had begun. Their personalities as well as their talents complemented each other. Right from the outset they won many hearts. News of the new owners spread quickly through the town and the district. John's detailed attention to organisation and efficiency; his business acumen, courtesy and friendliness combined with his innate selling ability ensured that the flow of customers would continue to increase. Mary's outgoing personality, her genuine desire to help others and her instant appeal to customers, particularly the women, who confided their many problems, had a similar effect. Enthusiasm and passion characterised everything they did. They learnt about the therapeutic benefits of healthy nutrition, of the function of vitamin and mineral supplementation and the importance of a balanced lifestyle in maintaining good health.

They went to in-service courses on natural health and healing at every opportunity and read widely from their substantial stock of health books. The early trading figures reflected their enthusiasm and hard work. John's innovative merchandising ideas: 'Opening Specials', 'Sale Table', 'VIP Customer Club' and sponsoring of community charities all contributed to making The Health Bug a thriving business. It had a lovely welcoming atmosphere.

The business had been theirs for almost four months when Hannah took part of her annual leave and came to stay with her parents for a few days. Her previous acquaintance with the shop had been on day visits. She walked around The Health Bug, stopping at each row of shelves, studying the array of vitamins, supplements, wholefoods (nuts, grains, seeds, dried fruits and various condiments) with child-like fascination.

'I never realised the huge variety of stock you carry here,' she said. 'Does all of this sell?'

'That's exactly what I wondered when I first saw this shop. When we came to do the stocktake before taking over, I asked Jack, the previous owner, about reducing the items. It's amazing that there were only a handful of items he said could go. He was quite right ... while some things sell much slower than others, nevertheless it all moves.'

That night over dinner the new business dominated the topic of conversation.

'You know, Hannah, it's just amazing what we've learnt about health and nutrition in the past three months ... now that I know what goes into nearly all the processed foods in the average supermarket trolley, I'm not surprised that doctors' surgeries are overflowing,' Mary said animatedly. 'In so many ways I'm finding this business is really changing my outlook on life', she went on, 'for example, I've never stopped to consider the extent of preservatives, colouring agents, additives and sugar in almost all of the food on the supermarket shelves ... the hyperactivity and ADD epidemic is hardly surprising ... nor is the increased incidence of chronic illnesses such as heart disease, diabetes and cancer.'

'Mum, you'll be writing the Health Column for *New Idea* soon,' Hannah said in mock-seriousness.

'Hannah, what I find exciting about this business is that not a day goes by when you don't learn something new ... This is all a new adventure for me ...'

'I'm so pleased to hear that you and Dad have taken so well to your new life. Frankly, I was somewhat apprehensive about you embarking into such uncharted territory.'

'We haven't really looked back, have we, dear?'

'No ... we're glad we made this break ... I've got no regrets at all ...', John said, sustaining Mary's positive tone.

'No more holidays, though ... how are you and Dad going to have a rest?', Hannah asked pensively.

'Well, Jack and Edna, the retired owners, are still around and have offered to run the shop if we need a break.'

'Oh well, I guess that's good to have in the back of your mind when the time comes.'

John ran each week and each month's figures off on the computer and compared the turnover with the same period in the preceding year. He was pleased with the outcome, particularly considering the tough economic times and the fact that the local pharmacy and supermarket both had large health food sections. By the first anniversary of their new life Mary had acquired two certificates in natural therapies—homoeopathy and vitamin supplements—which graced the shop wall. Further, she had enrolled in a distance education mode to study for a diploma in Herbal Medicine.

On one of Hannah's regular visits, Mary noticed that she wasn't quite herself. She seemed to look pale and appeared to be lacking in appetite. 'Are you looking after yourself properly, Hannah?'

'Of course I am, Mum . . . why do you ask?'

'Well, you've lost your appetite . . . you eat like a bird when you're home. You have been feeling alright, haven't you?' Mary asked, with a hint of worry in her voice.

'Well, I didn't want to mention it, but I haven't actually been 100% lately.'

'What's been the matter?'

'Oh . . . I just feel generally unwell.'

'Have you been to the doctor?'

'I saw him a couple of weeks ago . . . he sent me for some basic tests, but they didn't show anything.'

'And how are you feeling now?'

'So, so . . .'

'Hannah, please promise me that you'll go to the doctor without delay . . . promise?'

'I promise . . . but then you promise me you won't worry.'

Of course John and Mary did worry.

'I'm sure all those supplements you gave her should do the trick,' John reassured his wife.

'Let's hope so,' Mary said.

A few nights later the phone rang shortly after dinner. Mary answered it. 'Hannah, what's the news?'

John put his pen down from the daily banking and looked intently at his wife, whose anxiety he felt before he knew what it was all about. Mary's furrowed brow and short sharp breaths ignited his fear. He could barely contain his impatience to find out exactly what was wrong with his daughter.

'Listen . . . I'll arrange for Edna to work with Dad next week . . . yes, I want to . . . there's no question of anything else ... so don't go on. Look, darling, just don't worry ... our thoughts and prayers are with you ... you'll be OK ...'

The next few days marked a turning point in the Edwards' household.

Tests had led to urgent surgery, during which a cancerous tumour was removed from Hannah's right breast. This was followed by chemotherapy and radiation. Unfortunately, the cancer had metastasised and there were traces of lesions in her right lung and her liver.

The prognosis was poor. Mary and John organised for Jack and Edna, the former owners, to help in the shop while Mary went to be near the hospital. From the day of Hannah's diagnosis, Mary voraciously read everything she could lay her hands on about cancer. She went to the Cancer Information Society and read all about conventional and complementary treatments. Hannah took the news badly. She was devastated. In the early days she didn't want to see family and friends as she felt that she couldn't cope with their pity.

Mary's knowledge of vitamin and mineral supplements and their therapeutic value combined with an incredible coincidence. Only a few weeks before Hannah's diagnosis Mary had attended an international cancer congress sponsored by a large international vitamin company. The congress brought together many leading lights of the medical profession: those who represented both conventional and complementary therapies. This was the catalyst for Mary's iron determination to beat her daughter's illness. Having composed herself after the initial shock, Mary had a deep conviction that the remarkable recoveries she had heard and read about meant one thing—people *can* recover from cancer and they *have* recovered. If it has been achieved, she was going to do everything humanly possible to make sure that Hannah would be one of these remarkable people.

John also took the news of his daughter's illness badly. Fortunately, the shop, with its constant heavy demand on his time and energies, was a benefit as it cushioned his shock and gave him an outlet for his sorrow. He was deeply touched that so many of his loyal customers showed such concern for Hannah, even though, of course, they had never met her. John and Mary were heartened by the fact that this generosity of spirit, this solicitous concern was a measure of the esteem in which they were held in their customers' eyes.

Hannah came to convalesce following her release from hospital. She was to begin a seven-week program of radiotherapy shortly. Even before she came home from hospital Mary put all her reading and research into practice. She encouraged Hannah to be positive: 'Darling . . . together we're going to beat this . . . there was a purpose behind the timing of our purchase of this business.'

Through her tears and anguish, Mary was fiercely determined to fight this illness and win. Everything she read about the importance of having a strong belief in being able to get well; of having a strong faith in the treatment; of being spiritually strong; and the importance of emotional support was conveyed to Hannah. Mary persuaded Hannah to start a strict anti-cancer diet immediately. She also started a strict vegetable juicing regime, although not entirely without resistance.

'Mum, I can cope with carrot and celery but . . . really, this green juice . . . yuk . . . if this is the cure, then it's almost worse than the complaint . . .'

'As you drink it . . . visualise the chlorophyll and those wonderful enzymes oxygenating the blood and starving the cancer cells.'

Hannah began meditation and visualisation. She used tapes on guided imagery, on rapid relaxation and read about the ways these aspects of self-help mobilise the immune system. She joined a local cancer support group in Brighton. Meanwhile, John took her to the weekly sessions of radiotherapy in the city. From her reading Hannah taught herself to visualise the radiation targeting and killing off the weak, confused cancer cells. Although Hannah embraced the conventional treatment she was offered, her doctors were clear that with metastatic spread as extensive as hers she would be one of the lucky ones if her treatment were to be effective.

Hannah's recovery from the surgery went well. Mary had arranged for them to visit a GP in the city who also was a qualified naturopath. He fine-tuned Hannah's diet and her supplements and suggested a course of intravenous Vitamin C— a suggestion she followed.

When the radiation treatment stopped, Hannah had further tests. The comforting news was that no further spread had been detected. After a pause, Hannah began a lengthy course of chemotherapy. Hannah's oncologist was pleasantly surprised that her treatment had not given her the usual nasty side effects— at least, only in a limited way . . . for about an hour after each treatment.

'It's all this juicing, my diet and the vitamins and minerals I'm on,' Hannah told her oncologist.

He smiled benignly. 'Well, of course, there's no scientific evidence that dietary manipulations can alter the course of this disease but I don't want to discourage you from continuing what you're doing . . . if you're feeling better from doing this, then by all means keep on doing it.'

Following quite a thorough examination, Hannah asked if everything was all right.

'Yes . . . fine . . . what I would like you to do is to have another CT scan in a few weeks' time . . . in the meantime, we'll monitor the chemotherapy carefully and have another full blood test.'

Hannah avoided any mention of the intravenous C or the vitamin and mineral supplements she was taking. What was the point? It would have only antagonised him. After all, Dr Riley was a conventional medical scientist who had little time and even less inclination for the philosophy of 'holistic medicine.' His strict adherence was to a scientifically based medical model. The idea of the influence of the mind over the body, or of the nexus between emotional trauma and physical illness was beyond his ken. Nor, as Hannah discovered, did Dr Riley have any time for those who believed that 'dietary manipulations' or 'New Age mumbo jumbo' such as meditation could make one jot of difference to the outcome of cancer. The idea of the power of the body's immune system to mobilise its self-healing potential or the notion that people could do much to enhance their chances of survival, or even obtain a cure, was anathema to the likes of Dr Riley.

'You know, Mum, I would love to ask Dr Riley about his explanation of "spontaneous remission" but of course, I wouldn't dare,' Hannah told her mother one night over the dinner table. 'What a pity these doctors can't at least recognise the healing potential of conventional and complementary treatments that can come from a healing partnership.'

'Yes, I should present him with that book on remarkable recoveries from cancer. I mean . . . how would he explain them away?' Mary added.

'Mum, you don't really believe he'd actually read it, do you?'

'No, I guess that is being somewhat naive. On the other hand, I can't understand how someone of his intellect could deliberately ignore the differentiation between curing and healing an illness such as cancer . . . the notion that emotional suffering and pain will impede the healing process.'

'Well there have been no double blind studies done on it, have there, dear? It's so unfortunate that a person of his medical knowledge can't bring himself to admit . . . let alone believe, that we are a mind, body and spirit and that if any of these elements are suffering, then healing cannot take place.'

The months ahead saw a steady progress in Hannah's condition—a progress which amazed her doctors. Each blood test and CT scan brought encouraging news. Hannah set as one of her goals during visualisation to see herself healthy and back at work. She trod her healing path one step at a time; it was a steady walk of faith. Faith in her treatments, in her doctors, a new-found faith in a God she had long since abandoned. She had learnt to live in the moment, leaving fear aside. Her meditation was characterised by a deep conviction that healing was taking place. Her faith was fuelled by the deep love of her parents and in the boyfriend who had recently become her fiancé. Hannah's faith, her determination and self-discipline continued to yield their fruits. She faced each hurdle with equanimity and courage.

The first anniversary of the Edwards' family's take-over of The Health Bug came and went, overshadowed by the concern for Hannah. Not long after that anniversary, Hannah's doctors informed her that the way forward in terms of establishing precisely what the cancer was doing, was to undergo a relatively minor exploratory operation. At first Hannah was somewhat reluctant, but having a deep faith in her surgeon, she decided to go along with his advice. Her decision was vindicated. This time the news called for much thankfulness and jubilation. She was officially in remission. A new chapter in her healing journey had begun.

Paul Kraus

Your Emotions are Chemical

Laughter and joy can mean a healing, life-enhancing message going to every cell in your body, whereas shame, guilt and despair can lead to destructive messages. Your emotions are chemical. It is exciting to understand that specific thoughts can create changes in the body. When you are happy, your body knows it. When you're depressed and feeling hopeless, your body also knows that. And when I refer to your body I mean your bone marrow, the lining of your blood vessels, your liver. Every organ participates in the happiness or the sadness. It seems that consciousness and knowledge occur at the cell membrane. (Candace Pert, a neuro-physiologist, has done work with neuropeptides and in essence feels that awareness and consciousness will ultimately be located at the cell membrane.)

We know that the happy individual has a different set of neuropeptides (hormones) circulating from those of the person who is depressed, angry or anxious. Our nervous system and other organ systems through these neuropeptides are communicating with every cell in our bodies. Our gut feelings, how to deal with life, how many white cells we produce, how rapidly a wound heals—all these are linked.

Francis Hodgson Burnett describes this well in *The Secret Garden*:

> One of the new things people began to find out in the last century was that thoughts—just mere thoughts—are as powerful as electrical batteries—as good for one as sunlight is, or as bad for one as poison. To let a sad thought or a bad one get into your mind is as dangerous as letting a scarlet fever germ into your body. If you let it stay there after it has got in, you may never get over it as long as you live.

If you visualise a change happening in your body, (you don't have to know anatomy to create a satisfactory image), the body will respond. If you picture more blood going to your wounded leg, then indeed, more blood will flow there. The mind and body are not two separate entities, they are one; we are a unit.

In addition to our emotions, the mind and body also communicate through visualisation and meditation. These can provide another doorway to the unconscious, to our true path and healing . . .

One gentleman wrote to me about an experience he had had in hospital. The predictions were that he had about six months to live and that he should think about getting his affairs in order. This stripped away all of his hope. His doctor's prognosis was given in a small underground chamber, after which he was transported back to his hospital room through a long corridor: 'That ride became the visual and physical metaphor for my full recovery.'

He said that the first half of the passageway leading from the tumour institute to the hospital declined to a point midway, then turned to a slight incline as one approached the hospital: 'As I rode away from the institute on the down slope, there could not have been a lower emotional state. My life seemed to be caving in around me, yet just as we reached the lowest point of the passageway, I glanced ahead and realised that I was facing an upward climb. It was a small thing at the time, but it was the spark of hope and inspiration I needed. The uphill choice was mine and I chose to live. From then on, despite a second operation and six weeks of radiation, I knew in my heart I would return to full health.'

He is well twenty years later.

What is significant is what he 'knew in my heart.' It all starts with a belief—down to every cell in your body. You must believe to have it happen . . .

The mind, body and spirit are all integrated . . . We can allow ourselves to be empowered, to induce self-healing through the creative aspects of poetry, music, art and images and let them work within us to help cure our disease and heal our lives.

From Living, Loving and Healing *by Bernie Siegel, MD*
The Aquarian Press, (An imprint of
Harper Collins Publishers), London. 1993.
Used by permission.

The Healing Power of Love

We once saw a beautiful scene in a documentary about the life of Mother Teresa. She and several of her Sisters of Charity had appeared in Lebanon during the war, asking, 'How can we help?' They were sent to a home for spastic children that was short-staffed. The children there seemed small for their ages, shrunken and stunted. They were suffering from an illness known as hospitalism, or failure to thrive, that often occurs in group homes for infants. Although the children are fed and changed, their needs are met on schedule with little chance for the give and take that is natural between infant and caretaker. The pituitary glands of these unloved children fail to put out enough growth hormone. In effect, the baby gives itself a die message since there is no one to receive it into life.

Mother Teresa was holding one such child in the palm of her hand. The baby's face was squeezed into what looked like a death mask, and its shrivelled limbs were contorted in spasm. All she did was hold the baby and croon to it, looking at the child with great love. After a few moments, the baby began to smile, and its tortured limbs relaxed. When Mother Teresa was asked why she bothered to care for the sick and the dying since they had no hope of recovery, she replied that her job was simply to love them. That was enough.

Quoted from The Power of the Mind to Heal
by Joan and Miroslav Borysenko
Specialist Publications, Concord, NSW, Australia. 1995.
Used by permission.

LAUGHTER AND MUSIC

The Healing Benefits of Music

Down through the ages, many volumes have been written about this subject. Music and rhythm are built in to our nature. It only requires nurturing from a very young age to develop and enhance this gift. This was the central point made by the great violinist, Yehudi Menuhin, in a radio interview he gave on his last Australian visit in 1998. Menuhin's remarkable musical career, which spanned most of this century, is clear testimony to the fact that music is a universal language that transcends cultural barriers. The potential of music to assist in healing body, mind and spirit is great. What follows serves to suggest some of the more obvious healing properties of music, as well as briefly discussing the ways in which music works to help us maintain balance in our lives.

Music energises our soul and stirs our emotions, both individually and communally. It can calm us when we are annoyed or anxious, thus reducing our level of stress. Music can inspire us with hope when we are sad or lonely; it can help to clear our minds and can act as a catalyst for releasing our creative energies. Sometimes, if music is too loud, and we perceive it merely as an invasive noise, or when it is not to our taste, it can have negative mental and even physical effects. However, what positive effects can music have in assisting the healing process?

At an emotional and psychological level, music can alleviate loneliness. Pleasurable sounds tend to lift our spirits by taking us out of our situation and helping us to visualise a peaceful, happier environment. Music has been described as 'auditory colours.' In other words, music impacts upon our auditory senses in much the same way as colour does to our vision. Therefore, music helps to integrate our minds and bodies and can provide us with sources of inspiration and hope, by taking us out of our isolating silence. It can also provide us with positive, soothing thoughts and thus lift our mood. This alone has a number of direct beneficial physical effects. The first of these is that our endorphin levels are increased. In a layperson's language endorphins are the body's 'healing chemicals', which are triggered by positive emotions. As these hormones are released into the bloodstream, so our adrenalin level drops, as does our heart beat, pulse rate and blood pressure. Stress and its byproduct, muscular tension, are reduced. According to a number of scientific studies, soft relaxing music also promotes other hormones which tend to reduce our stress level.

When our stress is lowered, our immune function is heightened. This is achieved by a change in our metabolic rate, including lowered levels of respiration, thus increasing blood oxygen levels. Also, listening to pleasurable music has been shown to reduce levels of cortisol, a steroid hormone associated with the adrenal complex. Stress raises the level of cortisol and, if prolonged, can tend to exhaust our adrenal glands, thus reducing our immune response.

In many other ways, music assists in the healing process. Emotionally, physically and spiritually, pleasant music and sound contribute to healing. It holds a special place in people's lives—to many, music is a 'sacred' experience.

Music and Laughter

International research has shown that music and laughter have physiological and psychological benefits for those in need of healing. Music and laughter, in their distinctive ways, promote peace of mind, hope and, therefore, healing. Music can uplift the soul and sweep away our cares; it can be deeply relaxing; it can inspire love and compassion; music can enhance the healing powers of meditation and prayer. Sounds are an integral part of life. Long ago an unknown writer stated: 'A melody is like a friend without jealousy, without reservations, without expectations. Unconditionally, a melody can be a selfless ally when we're happy, a crutch when we're sad.'

It is fascinating to note that in Old English the origins of the word 'heal' refer to 'making sound', or to becoming healthy again. We hear of such phrases as 'sound judgment' or 'sound idea'. In this context the word 'sound' obviously means 'healthy'. Likewise, there are many other examples of words related to sound which are closely identified with the idea of health and healing. For example, we hear of 'setting the right tone', 'being on the same wavelength' or 'striking a sympathetic chord'.

One of the most inspiring things about music, laughter and meditation, as agents of healing, is that they are absolutely free and available to everyone.

The following three poems illustrate, albeit only partially, the therapeutic qualities of music and laughter.

Feasting

Rich and poor, Jew and Greek,
wise and foolish come—
invited by Johann Sebastian Bach
to share this feast
of Preludes, Toccatas,
Fantasias and Fugues.

A hush descends
and the feasting
begins with majestic
strains of a Prelude and Fugue
in the C major key.
This lyric of love
bursts forth
to sweep pestiferous
thoughts away.
Private griefs and cares
swamped
by effusive cadences,
coruscations and chromatic melodies
in sweet counterpoint.

This dialogue with the soul:
brief, yet unequivocal
in its triumphant affirmations.
What mind, what heart,
what virtuosity worked
these simple themes
into elaborations and configurations
which overpower the mind
and melt the heart?

Angelic voices from the Choir
sing praises,
while the sage Pedal
converses with the Great.

Trumpets intone eternal truths
amidst heavenly visions and crystal skies.
Toccata, Adagio and Fugue
with brilliant bravura lasts—
until the Adagio casts
an exquisite spell,
like a rainbow against purple sky.
Monumental chords
sabotage this hypnotic harmony
as they foretell
contrapuntal melodies
which vault the ceiling
of the mind
to cast their imprint
on the heart.

Paul Kraus

Piano Recital

Head bowed, prayerfully attuning mind
and heart to monumental task at hand.
Cosmic light magnifies the Steinway grand.
Hypnotic silence, then crisp chords sound,
heralding healing on eagle's wings.
Exalted, lofty scenery—
snapshot of eternity.

Chopin's trills and tremolos:
cascading, compelling, ravishing,
singing, leaping, rejoicing,
reviving the soul—
making it whole.
Variations and recapitulations,
gradations and modulations.
Echoes of light transform our fears,
fragrant chords dry our tears.

Beautiful Bach plunges unfathomable
depths, filling the mind with indomitable
thoughts of hope and victory,
knowing that time, that cruel commodity
is, after all, illusory.

Paul Kraus

Dr Fruit-Loop and Friends

for Dr Peter Spitzer and the Clown Doctors

One day each week—one special day—
Routine is left behind
for a little magic, fantasy and fun.
Dr Fruit-Loop and his Friends
introduce new guests into the Ward:
Uncle Fantasy and Aunty Fun,
Brother Empathy, Sister Sympathy
come helping wounded little hearts to heal.

Laughter and Happiness—mischievous twins,
(alias Doctors Sniggles and Bubba-Louie)
come crashing through the doors
spreading kinky kindness,
jollity and mirth,
like stardust through the Ward.

Amidst giggling, juggling, frolicking, tickling . . .
behind the magic, masks and mime,
the funny flasks, the coloured flowers . . .
lie the sadness and the solitude.

Too many sullen little faces
simply yearn to know why this is so.
Why are they lying there?
Why are they not elsewhere,
playing, laughing, enjoying the day?

The clown medicos soothe the hurt:
red nose transplants,
silly sounds of honking horns,
squeeking cat scans and funny-bone checks.

The nurse asks Dr Fruit-Loop and his Friends
'What works the best?'
Fruit Loop replies in a pensive tone:

'A tender smile, a tiny touch,
a twinkling eye ... a gentle hug ...
Silence of the unspoken word ...'
was all he said.

Paul Kraus

Tai Chi—A Brief Encounter

for Tibor

A gymnast's frame: strong,
muscular yet supple,
beguilingly agile;
Such graceful movements
in perfect synchronicity
with the sonorous harmony.

Peaceful interlude—
like a lullaby caressing the soul,
dispelling disturbing thoughts.
Profound tranquillity.
Words superfluous;
this healing spell, like precious balm,
soothing the heart.

At last he speaks ... gently, but boldly,
like an evangelist proclaiming good news
to those believing that healing
comes from within;
from hearts and minds,
affirming the power of positive thoughts.

His gospel proclaims
that sickness is an anomaly.
His message, almost a parody,
'This body is a precious gift—
sustain and nourish it with good food;
learn to breathe, to have balance in your life.
The body seeks to heal itself—
allow it the chance so to do;
to restore its balance, to gradually
revive, regenerate and repair.

Take care to rest mind and body.
Surrender negativity, cultivate positivity,
restore the rhythms of your life.
Only then can you invigorate your soul,
and find your healing path.'

Paul Kraus

The Power of Music and Laughter to Transform

The following extract from Norman Cousins' best-selling book about the nature of healing and regeneration, Anatomy of an Illness, *recounts the healing and revitalising effect of music on a famous musician, the cellist Pablo Cassals, who was an old, rather sick and frail man when Cousins met him. Cousins describes the remarkable therapeutic effect that creating music had on this elderly man who was suffering from rheumatoid arthritis and emphysema and was badly stooped. In a very real sense, music was his medicine. Music uplifted him in mind and body. This account describes how Cousins witnessed this take place during a visit to the great musician.*

Even before going to the breakfast table, Pablo went to the piano—which I learned was a daily ritual. He arranged himself with some difficulty on the piano bench, then with discernible effort raised his swollen and clenched fingers above the keyboard. I was not prepared for the miracle that was about to happen. The fingers slowly unlocked and reached toward the keys like the buds of a plant toward the sunlight. His back straightened. He seemed to breathe more freely. Now his fingers rolled on the keys. Then came the opening bars of Bach's Wohltemperierte Klavier, played with great sensitivity and control. I had forgotten that Pablo had achieved proficiency on several instruments before he took up the cello. He hummed as he played, then said that Bach spoke to him here—and he placed his hand over his heart.

Then he plunged into a Brahms concerto and his fingers, now agile and powerful, raced across the keyboard with dazzling speed. His entire body seemed fused with the music; it was no longer stiff and shrunken but supple and graceful and completely freed from its arthritic coils. Having finished the piece, he stood up by himself, far straighter and taller than he had when he came into the room . . .

Laughter and humour, in a similar way to music, are therapeutic in their effects on body, mind and spirit. Considerable research in recent years has substantiated this belief into fact. As to how laughter and humour work on the mind and body is not fully known. The evidence clearly shows that neuropeptides called endorphins are released by the brain. These work favourably on the endocrine system and the adrenal glands to enhance the body's immune function. The following extract also comes from Anatomy of an Illness *and is a very readable account of the connection between humour and wellness.*

The Bible tells us that a merry heart works like a doctor. Exactly what happens inside the human mind and body as the result of humour is difficult to say. But the evidence that it works has stimulated the speculation not just of physicians but of philosophers and scholars over the centuries. Sir Francis Bacon called attention to the physiological characteristics of mirth. Robert Burton, in his *Anatomy of Melancholy* almost four hundred years ago, cited authorities for his observation that 'humour purges the blood, making the body young, lively and fit for any manner of employment'. In general, Burton said, mirth is the 'principal engine for battering the walls of melancholy . . . and a sufficient cure in itself'. Hobbes describes laughter as a 'passion of sudden glory'.

Immanuel Kant, in his *Critique of Pure Reason*, wrote that laughter produces a 'feeling of health through the furtherance of the vital bodily processes, the affection that moves the intestines and the diaphragms; in a word, the feeling of health that makes up the gratification felt by us; so that we can thus reach the body through the soul and use the latter as the physician of the former'. If Kant was intimating that he never knew a man who possessed the gift of hearty laughter to be burdened by constipation, I can readily agree with him. It has always seemed to me that hearty laughter is a good way to jog internally without having to go outdoors.

Sigmund Freud's fascination with the human mind was not confined to its malfunctioning or its torments. His researches were directed to the supremely mysterious station occupied by the brain in the universe. Wit and humour to him were highly differentiated manifestations of the uniqueness of the mind. He believed that mirth was a highly useful way of counteracting nervous tension, and that humour could be used as effective therapy . . .

. . . Current scientific research in the physiological benefits of laughter may not be abundant but is significant nonetheless . . .

Some people, in the grip of uncontrollable laughter, say their ribs are hurting. The expression is probably accurate, but it is a delightful 'hurt' that leaves the individual relaxed almost to the point of a sprawl. It is the kind of 'pain', too, that most people would do well to experience every day of their lives. It is as specific and tangible as any other form of physical exercise. Though its biochemical manifestations have yet to be as explicitly charted and understood as the effects of fear or frustration or rage, they are real enough.

Increasingly, in the medical press, articles are being published about the high cost of the negative emotions. Cancer, in particular, has been connected to intensive states of grief or anger or fear. It makes little sense to suppose that emotions exact only penalties and confer no benefits . . . I became convinced that creativity, the will to live, hope, faith and love have biochemical significance and contribute strongly to healing and to well-being. The positive emotions are life-giving experiences.

From Anatomy of an Illness *by Norman Cousins*
Bantam Books, New York, 1981.

MEDITATION

A Technique to Break the Addiction of Thought

Meditation is a technique to break the addiction of thought; in essence it is directed concentration. By sitting and trying to maintain the focus of concentration on some object—the breath, body sensations, a visual image—you learn to control attention and keep it in one place. Meditation practice is both simple and difficult: simple because the method is nothing more than maintaining focused attention; difficult because it requires changing lifelong habits of letting the mind wander where it will, especially into thoughts. Even when you learn to sit motionless for a half-hour and mostly keep your attention on your chosen object of meditation, you may not be able to extend that successful calming and focusing into the rest of your life.

The real goal of meditation practice is to do it constantly, to practice meditation in action as you move through the world. Even if you are not ready to undertake that sort of training, you can begin by trying to move your attention to your body or your breath whenever you remember to do so, especially when you notice that your mind has been led away from the here and now by the endlessly fascinating process of thought.

Excerpt from Spontaneous Healing *by Andrew Weil, MD*
Ballantine Publishing Group, New York, 1995.
Used with permission.

The Silent Healer

As an aid to recovering from a major illness such as cancer, meditation has been shown to be a powerful 'silent healer'. The late Dr Ainslie Meares, a Melbourne psychiatrist, was a pioneer in promoting the health-giving possibilities of meditation. More recently, much of Ian Gawler's work with cancer patients has centred on using meditation as a tool to aid in improving patients' quality of life and to assist in the recovery process.

The practice of meditation has a history which spans many centuries in both Eastern and Western philosophies. Unfortunately, many people shy away from both the idea and practice of meditating because they perceive meditation as being identified with mysticism or religion. They fail to realise that meditation is a practice which can be done quite independently of any religious belief. It is a wonderful remedy for stress and for bringing the body into a state of deep relaxation. When the body is deeply relaxed its capacity for self-healing is enhanced.

The following poems attempt not only to define what meditation is, but to convey what it is that makes meditation such an effective tool for healing—for bringing the body into a state of balance.

Meditation

for Col Douglass

Warning bells
ring false alarms
to ignorant minds,
as once they did
in mine.
Fickle winds
of prejudice
blew meditation
beyond my reach.
Until one day
Circumstance
cruelly intervened.

'Cancer is a Word,
not a Sentence,'
they told me ...
That fearful Word
which held me
in its vice-like grip.

Softly and gently
Meditation beckoned:
'Try my healing power',
it gently called.
My mind wavered
like a summer breeze.
Imperceptibly,
meditation massaged
my fear away.

Knowledge ... no,
... a state of mind,
simply, effortlessly
gained, so effortlessly ...
just so effortlessly
showed meditation
enhancing the healing
power of prayer.

Paul Kraus

The ABC of Meditating

for Ian Gawler

Abandoning ... self ... stress ... and ... fear ...
Accepting ... the moment ... living in peace ...
Affirming ... positive thoughts ...
Balancing ... the body's biochemistry ...
Becalming ... the mind ...
Breathing ... lifeline of consciousness ...
Calming ... the strife within ...
Ceasing ... all noise ... like clouds ... thoughts quickly pass ...
Celestial sound ... of silence ...
Deepening ... our response ... relaxing ...
Deeper ... and deeper ... into the ... quietness ...
Defeating ... dreaded fear
Enchanting ... silence ...
Endorphins ... releasing ...
Experiencing ... such healing harmony ...
Fear ... now going ...
Feeling ... good ...
Finding ... my soul ...
Going with it ... just simply letting go ...
Good feeling ... this letting go ...
Healing ... the damage ...
Heightening ... experience ...
Immediate ... soothing ... softening ...
Intentionally ... relaxing ...
Just ... letting go ...
Just ... simply ... letting go ...
Knowing ... yet not knowing ...
Knowing ... only goodness ...
Leaving ... behind ... stress ...
Loving ... the moment ...
Meditating ... regularly ...
Muscles ... softening ... loosening ...
No hurry ... no worry ...

Nowhere ... to go ... nothing else to do ...
Our ... thoughts turn inward ...
Our ... hearts grow warm ...
Persevering ... with it ... persisting ...
Praying ... listening ... in sweet silence ...
Questioning ... ceases ... silence sustaining ... the peace
   within ...
Questions ... abandoned ... going with it ...
Relaxing ... softening ... loosening ...
Releasing ... the tension ... simply letting go ...
Sighing ... it's good to sigh ... they say ...
Simply ... letting go ...
The ... numinous appearing ... splendid visions ...
Transcendental ... experience ...
Unloading ... burdens ...
Uplifted ... into ... a celestial realm ...
Vanquishing ... fear ...
Visualising ... healing ...
Words ... abandoned ...
Worry ... forgotten ...
Xylophones ... softly ... sweetly playing ...
Yet ... a new ...
Zeal ... for life ... like ...
Zephyrs ... uplifting ... hope ... restoring.

Paul Kraus

Dialogues on the Nature of Meditation and Its Relevance to Healing

Dr Ainslie Meares (1910–1986) was an eminent Australian psychiatrist. He had been President of the International Society for Clinical and Experimental Hypnosis and a Foundation Fellow of the Royal Australian and New Zealand College of Psychiatrists. He worked in psychotherapy with the paintings of schizophrenic patients and became well-known in medical circles for his pioneering work on hypnosis. He also worked extensively with meditation in the treatment of psychoneurotic and psychosomatic illness. He was a prolific author, having written twenty-seven books dealing with technical and popular aspects of psychiatry. He was also the author of numerous scientific papers. At the end of his career and in retirement, Dr Meares worked extensively on the effect of intensive meditation on cancer growth.

A number of his popular books were written in verse, because poetry evokes thoughts and emotions more directly than prose. The following eight 'poems' are what Dr Meares called dialogues on the nature of meditation.

(1) It all seems so simple;
     There must be something about it
     Which I do not grasp.

             If you grasp that it is simple,
             You grasp it all.

(2) Is it not that meditation
     And the beneficial effects
     Which you describe
     Are simply mysticism?
     If so, it's not for me.
     One thing I prize
     And that's the truth
     Of what is real.

Can you not see
There's a reality basis
For mysticism?
It's simply letting our mind
Work in another way.

(3) From the way you speak
I sense you feel
Some kind of poetry in it.

Poetry is not the words,
It is what they evoke.

(4) It seems to me
You cloud in mystery
Something
Which is in fact
Quite simple.

Simple it is.
But there's the mystery
For those whose vision
Has not learned to penetrate
The depth
Of such simplicity.

(5) As I see it,
Meditation is the last resource
For those who cannot cope with life.
I'm not in that class.
I cope.
In fact, I have no doubt I cope quite well.
What then has meditation got for me?

Nothing.
Doubt is the door
By which the light of knowledge
Enters our being.

Until you learn to doubt,
Don't come to me.

(6) I say
I want peace of mind.
You say
Just meditate.
Is it as simple as all that?

Not quite
And that's not quite what I say.
More than meditate
Let the effect of it
Flow through our life.

(7) I sometimes wish
I were closer to God.

It may well be true
That God
Is in the noise and the bustle,
But perhaps
It is easier to find Him
In the calm and the stillness.

(8) Is meditation
Akin to prayer?

It is,
If you make it so.

Taken from Dialogue on Meditation,
From the Quiet Place, A Kind of Believing
by Ainslie Meares
Hill of Content Publishing, Melbourne, 1989.
Used with permission.

When You Meditate

When you meditate, be like a mountain
immovably set in silence.
Its thoughts are rooted in eternity.
Do not do anything, just sit, be
and you will reap the fruit flowing from
your prayer.

When you meditate, be like a flower
always directed towards the sun.
Its stalk, like a spine, is always straight.
Be open, ready to accept everything without fear
and you will not lack light on your way.

When you meditate, be like an ocean
always immovable in its depth.
Its waves come and go.
Be calm in your heart
and evil thoughts will go away by themselves.

When you meditate, remember your breath:
thanks to it we are alive.
It comes from God and it returns to God.
Unite the word of prayer with the stream of life
and nothing will separate you from the
Giver of life.

When you meditate, be like a bird
singing without a rest in front of the Creator.
Its song rises like the smoke of incense.
Let your prayer be like the coo of a dove
and you will never succumb to discouragement.

Every mountain teaches us the sense of eternity
every flower, when it fades,
teaches us the sense of fleetingness.
The ocean teaches us how to retain peace
among adversities,
and love always teaches us Love.

Fr Seraphion of Mount Athos
(Adapted by Fr Jan Bereza, OSB)

LETTING GO …
OF RESENTMENT,
NEGATIVITY AND FEAR

Letting Go

An interesting common thread in the stories of cancer patients is that frequently they tell of years of unresolved or repressed negative emotions, such as guilt, resentment, bitterness or fear. 'Letting go' refers to the ability to be able to shed such negativity and become 'whole' and achieve balance in one's life again. Sometimes a person's inability to be able to do this over a prolonged period can actually lead to illness. This inability to 'let go' is usually the result of problems with personal relationships.

The following poems and the story, 'A Gradual Healing' represent very different aspects of 'letting go'. The first poem describes a cathartic experience, a purging of residual negativity— of resolving past conflicts. The second poem is about a very different type of 'letting go'. In the first half of this sonnet the poet is puzzling over the direction his life has been taking. It is a direction which has left him with a sense of hopelessness. In the last six lines he surveys the awesome beauty around him. This enables him to 'let go' and see everything in an altogether different perspective.

My Father

Many years have passed since he died.
My children, infants then
are now young men.
Many times I counted
him among the living dead.
He lived for work
not worked to live.
Estranged, fatigued,
ensnared, trapped
like a prisoner
in solitary confinement
whose children led
their lives in sweet oblivion
of their father's daily grind.

In the cauldron of my rebellious heart
emotional conflicts seethed:
resentment, strangeness
and stern rebukes
at our ingratitude.
His foreignness
my chief embarrassment.

Middle age returns
my thoughts
to him again.
Sadly now his sufferings
refracted in a different light.
His torments, hurts and sorrows
then hidden from my youthful eyes.

Beyond his tenacity to succeed
lay a deep humanity
and magnanimity
which healed past hurts,
redeemed lost time,

resolved much bitterness
and wrangles from the past.
Negative feelings
long since purged
by time . . .
and tender thoughts.

Paul Kraus

Twilight—South Head Lighthouse

'What is man, that you are mindful of him?'
The psalmist pleaded in his despair.
The grandeur, this aura around
reanimates this refrain as I struggle
to understand the confusion in my soul.
The sound of crashing sea, the whistling of the wind,
the magic of this twilight hour
speaks in transcendental tones:

Worry not, nor grieve ambition lost in
this mad race for avaricious greed.
This adoration, this contemplation has freed
my mind from self and revealed riches not yet seen.
Wisdom, smashed like the waves on the rocks below,
Humanity's greatness, like a chimera in this evening glow.

Paul Kraus

A Gradual Healing

The sandstone of the chapel with its magnificent stained-glass window created a warm, mellow ambience in total contrast to the heat outside and the cobalt blue of this early December afternoon sky. The sanctity of this atmosphere is almost palpable. It is as if the stones themselves are suffused with prayer.

I genuflected before the altar, sank to my knees, sighed one of those 'letting go' sighs and allowed discursive thoughts time to subside. As the silence enveloped me I felt a wave of peace and calm. A year ago this place had felt so strange; now, it was a central part of my life. Inexpressibly, almost transcendentally, a great invigorating calm, like a pervasive sweet fragrance, revived me from my weariness. In the last few weeks of term the year had begun to feel like the closing stages of a marathon.

I sat up and slowly looked around, contemplating the intricate beauty of my surroundings: the soft glow of the Sanctuary lamp harmoniously blending with the white marble altar and the shining gold of the Tabernacle; the purple of the Advent altar cloth complementing the perfect symmetry of colour and light. Unwittingly, I had knelt alongside the Sixth Station of the Cross: Veronica wiping the face of Jesus. The sculptor capturing Grief, Compassion, Love so abundantly as if to remind me that I was surrounded by a religion of the heart, as much as of the mind; of the senses, as of the will. As I contemplated my surrounds, Jesus' words filled my mind: 'Come unto me, all who labour and are heavy laden, and I will give you rest ... for my yoke is easy and my burden is light.'

Tiredness and gratitude merged. Almost in disbelief I realised that it was one year to the day since first setting foot in this place when Father Jones interviewed me. I recalled the ripple of excitement I felt when he had phoned me on the very day he received my application. I realised also that it was exactly six months since I relinquished the faith into which I had been born, and, till recently, had been my livelihood. What a strange road I had travelled lately! Totally alien territory to my nearest

127

and dearest in life. Such an incomprehensible journey as far as they were concerned.

Twelve months ago I had few gleanings of the way in which this college was to totally dominate my life. It had become my home, my means of sustenance, and my spiritual lifeline as well. Suddenly, I felt as though I were in a time-warp, as I recalled my first encounter with Father Jones this day last year. The very words of that interview echoed in my mind:

'Do come in and take a seat, Mr Harrington' ... recollections of his spacious office with a woodcarving of St Ignatius' famous prayer of self-offering sitting on his large tidy desk. My eyes scanned its words as he hesitated before the interview, while finding my application. *Take my freedom, my memory, my understanding and my will . . . Give me only your love and grace . . .*

'I must say, Mr Harrington, that your application really stood out from the rest.'

'Thank you,' I replied diffidently.

'In fact, it is very rare to have an application with academic qualifications which include honours in both Arts and Theology. In a Jesuit college like this it is rarer still to have a former Anglican clergyman applying for a teaching position. Some years ago we had a Uniting Church minister on the staff, but I cannot recall someone with your background.'

I smiled but managed to refrain from speaking. I reminded myself of my resolve to let Father Jones take the initiative in the interview, to speak only when asked.

My initial tenseness quickly dissipated as I realised the kind of person I was facing—one who was taking pains to assure me that I was speaking to a fellow pilgrim, not specifically to a potential employer. Yet, quite unexpectedly, his next statement caught me unprepared.

'Do tell me a little more about your background, Mr Harrington.'

My years as a clergyman, counselling people, and learning to be a good listener suddenly served me poorly as I began trying to convey as best I could the momentous events of the past year which had culminated in this application.

'As you can see from my CV I had a traditional Anglican upbringing, culminating in ordination to the ministry. I guess that there was a certain predictability about it all, having been brought up in a Rectory and having an Anglican schooling. I sometimes believe that I drifted into the ministry—a natural progression, you might say, from school, university, then theological college. The Church was where I lived, moved and had my being. That being the case, my decision to leave the ministry and the Church was the loneliest and most painful of my life; made even more so by the unfortunate recent event in my domestic situation. Yet, I had no option but to be true to my conscience ... I'm afraid that my school teaching experience is limited to a stint at the Church of England Grammar School.'

Father Jones sat absorbed in what I was saying. We had moved away from his desk and were sitting on comfortable thickly padded chairs at one end of his study. It was a relaxed, non-threatening situation. 'Your story is intriguing, Mr Harrington,' he nodded, as if in empathy with all that I had just said.

'Your strong academic credentials are certainly impressive. You are probably aware of the importance a Jesuit College like ours places on scholarship and academic achievement. I am sure that not only the History Department, but all of us would benefit from having someone of your calibre on our staff ... but you realise, Mr Harrington, that we don't just take boys on academic merit and that we have our fair share of students whose interests are on the sporting field rather than in the classroom ... Academic reputation is all well and good, but the day-to-day reality of the classroom is another ... some of our lads are very trying, even for the most innovative of teachers.'

'I fully understand what you are suggesting, Father. Be assured, I have few illusions about the arduous nature of teaching.'

'Yes, Mr Harrington ... and it's not only the teaching that makes this job arduous, it's the fact that during term you are taking on a twenty-four-hours-a-day task. There's not much respite at all ... of course, you would have the occasional weekend off, but by and large, you have little time to yourself ... how would you feel about such a radical change to the lifestyle to which you have been accustomed?'

'I appreciate the balanced and candid way you present the task, Father. I have given much thought and prayer to this application. I realised right from the start that the position would be, to put it euphemistically, challenging. I also happen to believe that God never gives us a challenge without giving us the strength to cope with it . . . yes, just adjusting to such a radically new lifestyle is, in itself, a considerable challenge, but it's a challenge that I would eagerly anticipate . . . indeed, relish.'

Father Jones must have liked what I said. He went on to detail the exact requirements of the position, handing me a full job description.

'Spend a few moments looking at this sheet and see what you think.'

I perused the detailed job description. As I finished reading the page, he began to speak, 'Of course, it's not *quite* as onerous as described, but we're obliged to dot our 'I's and cross our 'T's.'

I nodded, somewhat feebly. He asked me a few more questions about my sporting and other interests, about my tastes in reading and music, and gradually, as the interview, which had become a convivial chat by now, wore on, I felt that I was talking to a kindred spirit. I sensed that the feeling was mutual. There was something more. In spite of our entirely different backgrounds, I could tell that he closely identified with the emotional pain which was still so much part of my daily existence.

Within a few days I received a formal letter offering me the position. I felt a surge of thankfulness and a feeling of elation as I opened the envelope and began to read:

Dear Mr Harrington
Thank you for attending the interview for the position of History Teacher/Assistant House Master . . . I enjoyed meeting you . . . I feel that we have much in common . . . and that not only would the College benefit from your presence with us, but that I would value the contribution I know you could undoubtedly make . . . I am pleased to advise you that you

have been appointed to our staff . . . Could you please let my secretary know of your intention to accept this offer . . .

Yours sincerely

(Fr) Tony Jones

I remember reading and re-reading the letter offering me the job. My heart was touched by euphoria. Almost magically, this short letter was the instrument which was about to set my life on an entirely new course. It was a strong impetus to heal the hurts of recent times.

The initial excitement was quickly tempered as I recalled Father Jones' words about the hard-nosed realities of College life. I realised afresh that the year ahead was going to be anything but easy, especially so because of the unfamiliarity of my new milieu. It would be a matter of taking each day as it came and walking by faith, not by sight. I was aware of the many problems inherent in a boarding school environment, especially those stemming from the emotional deprivation felt by many of the students—deprivations which compounded the normal difficulties of adolescence. Then, there was still the pain caused by my ten years of marriage having recently ended. On some days that wound was hard to bear. What could possibly compensate for my sense of betrayal and anguish?

As I sat in that magnificent chapel, the highlights of these past momentous twelve months flashed through my mind like sequences from a documentary. There was a pervading sense of disbelief . . . yes, a whole year since this new life began and a mere ten months since this place had actually become my home. Then the realisation that this was the first day I had sat and meditated upon the ways in which this place had changed me.

The school is eerily quiet now . . . the crowded year has run its course. The strangeness of my Jesuit milieu is strange no more. I have been, more or less, enculturated into its peculiarities, including witnessing the odd peccadilloes, as well as the virtues, of my Jesuit colleagues—and what oddities some of them were!

The word 'community' rings now with connotations it had never had for me in earlier times.

In hindsight, Father Jones' words a year ago appear prophetic. The steady stream of problems never stopped; some trivial, others not so, but ever omnipresent. His wise counsel about the emotional investment required of this position proved so accurate. Yet, beyond the difficulties lay rich rewards which only now— having left the hurly-burly of the daily rounds behind, I can appreciate. The greatest of these rewards was the gratitude— which I received in different, at times strange guises, from the boys. Another good thing had been the friendships I had formed with a couple of my teaching colleagues and the emotional support that came with these friendships. Foremost among these friendships was that of my House Master, Peter Hill. We quickly discovered that we had much in common, despite our differing backgrounds.

We were about the same age and we had both been to Sydney University at the same time. Peter had been on the staff for twelve years. His dedication to the school was complete, so I found it rather strange that he spoke with such detachment about it when I first met him.

'Yes, you must try not to let this place get to you . . . amidst the rough and tumble of each term, try to see the funny side of things . . . taking this place too seriously is not a good thing to do . . . not at all a healthy thing . . . try to remember that some of our lads, likeable as they are, have brains the size of pea hens . . . also, it's good to know which deadlines can be broken and which can't . . .'

As a raconteur of school life, Peter was brilliant. His impersonations, no less than his dry wit often left me sore from laughter. He was a walking *Dictionary of Quotations*. He seemed to always have the right quote for the right time, be it serious or humorous; and there was invariably a wisdom in whatever he said. He was a widely read man and was possessed of a rare saintly quality. Right from the beginning I valued his friendship and counted it an enriching experience. Among many other things, he took me out of the straitjacket of my Calvinistic thinking. In some ways he was a very private man and it was only late in second term that I discovered that he had been a priest for a short while before changing his vocation. Some evenings and weekends we idled away an hour or more chatting about poetry (or what passes for poetry in the literary journals these days), or, another of his favourite topics, Church politics, about which he mistakenly believed, I was knowledgeable. Occasionally, we had time for a game of chess or chatted over an interesting article or book we had come across in the library or at the local book shop.

The roller-coaster of the year, which seemed to gain momentum as the year progressed, has suddenly run its course. Stopped. Almost by way of anti-climax, the long-awaited holidays have arrived. Exams have been set and marked; reports written; registers brought up to date; the paper war won. The college is ghostly quiet, emptied of the familiar sounds of term. The recalcitrant hounds of the junior division have broken the leash and vanished—to their master's relief. Yet, the rhythm of the year still reverberates within, the 'unwinding' has only begun.

This chapel, this oasis in the college is like a healing balm for my soul; its silence so soothing. Today, as a year earlier, a gentle wave of peace washes over me. The sadness has ebbed away; the fears of the future gone. I feel wonderfully free. As I take my leave my eyes again catch those familiar words which have become my own: 'My yoke is easy and my burden light . . .'

Paul Kraus

Convalescence

Illness can be viewed as a turning point, a chance to change old ways, to let go and to make a new beginning. The following poem by the well-known Australian poet, Peter Skrzynecki, is one in a series about his own illness, which resulted in heart-bypass surgery. There is a deep poignancy in the way he talks about his new lease on life in the last two stanzas. The poem clearly shows the poet's acknowledgement of the positive effects his illness had on him. It is reproduced here with permission.

He knows there'll be times when he
starts feeling depressed—sorry for himself
and guilty at what he's done to the family:
to his wife and children, his aged parents,
the friends that sent flowers
or commiserations in cards and letters.

Often he loses track of days and dates,
what people have told him five minutes ago—
   asked when he will be returning to work,
the names of books he'd like them to bring.
Once, he remembers and laughs about it,
he even forgot his own name.

Going for walks in the early mornings
brings a freshness of sights, sounds and smells
as though he was encountering it all for the first time in his
    life:
        camelias, azaleas,
hawthorns, spikes of scarlet bottlebrush,
the drenching scent of wisteria trailing on fences—
silvereyes darting in and out of japonicas
or through the glory of Chinese Lanterns hung with dew.

But the soft tom-tom thud of his mended heart
tells him all's well, that he's alive and breathing—
to walk calmly, cherish the earth he's on,

to let go of old sorrows, grievances, regrets
and accept his new life with gratitude and love:

even though he might yearn and look back
for the winged freedom of silvereyes—
or the realms of an eternity he caught sight of
in a Chinese Lantern's golden fire.

Peter Skrzynecki

Decide to Forgive

In order to allow healing to take place—physical, emotional or spiritual—it is important that we try to release the poisonous effects of negative emotions, such as bitterness, resentment and guilt, by forgiving. Admittedly, this is something which we can't always do ourselves, particularly if the hurt is very great. In that case we need to talk it over with someone who is a good listener. If, for whatever reason, we persist with our grudges, then ultimately we will do ourselves great harm. Under those circumstances, healing cannot take place. The following short verse illustrates this idea and captures the benefits of releasing our negative emotions.

For resentment is negative
Resentment is poisonous
Resentment diminishes
and devours the self.
Be the first to forgive
To smile and take the first step
And you will see happiness bloom
On the face of your human
brother or sister.

Be always the first
Do not wait for others to forgive
For by forgiving
You become the master of fate
The fashioner of life
The doer of miracles

To forgive is the highest
most beautiful form of love.

In return you will receive
untold peace and happiness.

From Decide to Forgive *by*
Dr Robert Muller of the United Nations.
Reproduced with permission.

For Everything There is a Season

Life is often mysterious and complex—full of questions. This is preeminently so in the realm of suffering and healing. We do not know why some people are healed of an illness, while others are not. In this life we can never fully understand the nature and purpose of suffering. Those of us who have a firm faith and trust in God must know that His ways are not our ways and His thoughts are not our thoughts. The most comforting thought we could possibly have is that He will heal in the way He knows best. One of the Bible's most profound statements on suffering is found in the Book of Ecclesiastes in the Old Testament. In these brief, but profound statements we begin to understand the meaning of 'Letting Go and Letting God'. That does not mean a fatalistic, stoic acceptance of whatever happens to us; what it does mean is that only God, our loving Father, knows the ultimate purpose of events such as illness and suffering in our lives. We need to try to accept that everything in this world has a time and a place.

For everything there is a season,
and a time for every matter under heaven:
a time to be born, and a time to die;
a time to sow, and a time to reap;
a time to kill, and a time to heal;
a time to tear down, and a time to build up;
a time to weep, and a time to laugh;
a time to mourn, and a time to dance;
a time to cast away stones, and a time to gather stones
    together;
a time to embrace, and a time to refrain from embracing;
a time to seek, and a time to lose;
a time to keep, and a time to cast away;
a time to rend, and a time to sew;
a time to keep silence, and a time to speak;
a time to love, and a time to hate;
a time for war, and a time for peace ...

He has made everything beautiful in its time;
also He has put eternity into man's mind . . .

The Book of Ecclesiastes, Chapter 3, 1–8; 11

PEOPLE

The Influence of People

It is a truism that the people with whom we come into contact can deeply influence the way we feel. This is particularly so with those who are going through an illness. The following profile and poem illustrate this by their focus on a diverse range of emotions and situations. This section is an attempt to show us how important it is for our health and well-being to be aware of the positive influence people have on us and how others can show us courage, hope, laughter and positive thinking.

Jim Malliaros

This testimony is about a remarkable long-term cancer survivor. It is included here to show the powerful mind–body connection and the strength of the human spirit. This story also vividly illustrates the way in which emotions such as love and happiness have a positive role to play in maintaining health, even in the face of a life-threatening illness.

Jim was diagnosed on August 9th, 1984 as having terminal cancer of the prostate gland. It had spread to his spine, pelvis and the back of the ribs. Jim's future was bleak and it affected him badly. In his own words:

'Like most people who have been told that they face a situation similar to mine, the idea of cancer inevitably meant death. Death was to me a subject I associated with other people; the old, the sick or the lonely, and like most people I took it for granted. However when I was told that death was a real possibility in the very near future my initial shock was great— my health in the past had never been of any real concern.

'The next few weeks were spent with each day meaning that I was closer to death than the day before. My whole lifestyle seemed to be one of "no future"; I felt as if I had nothing to live for and sometimes I felt as though I might as well die now to stop all the suffering of the days ahead.

'Because of their situation with forthcoming exams, my wife and I decided against telling our two teenage children; however they too soon discovered the change in my way of life and we knew the news should be broken soon. My wife tried very hard to provide the love and attention to myself (to whom the doctors had given no hope) but the word "cancer" was taboo and we tried to ignore it.

'One day while at the newsagency (about three months after my diagnosis) I noticed a book near the newspaper I was going to buy called *You Can Conquer Cancer*. I decided to buy it and after reading only the first few pages my initial thoughts centred around the idea of "If he can do it, then so can I". Through the book and all that it had to offer, I became aware of The Australian Cancer Patients Foundation and so I quickly enrolled as a member and joined a particular group.

'What I learned at the Centre was:
- Hope: I began to think of the future, not just sickness and death.
- Understanding: I talked with people in the same position.
- Encouragement: I met people who had beaten cancer.
- Positive thinking: and the powers of the mind.
- Meditation: which helps my healing process.
- Diet: which promotes health of the body.

and most importantly:
- Happiness: (as a result of all the above): which had not been a part of my life for quite a while.

This ability to control and cope with stress and illness through meditation, diet and positive thinking has given me a new identity and now even my family are eating the type of food that I eat and are meditating with me. They say that they too have discovered more about life and themselves as a result of their and my "improved lifestyle".'

Jim has become keen to help others now he is feeling so much better. Greek born, Jim has visited several other Greek cancer patients and has been able to overcome the language barrier that sometimes exists for these people. Now Jim's ever-ready wit is helping others to laugh and look on the bright side, and he is an inspiration to many.

Jim has the wonderful gift of being able to share his positive experiences with others.

October 1985

August 1986—An Update
Jim has some insights to add now:

Jim says that 'initially I had a big problem in attending Ian's talks. On the one hand I knew that I had the best doctors and they were saying there was no hope for me. Yet here it all seemed so simple. When I started the course I found the first

143

three or four lessons unconvincing and because of this I did not believe Ian's ideas and methods would help me to cure my cancer. However, after a few more lessons, I slowly started to become convinced. By this stage, all the people in the group started talking freely to each other about their problems which helped enormously in our friendship and made all of us extremely happy.'

During 1985 Jim kept coming to The Gawler Foundation, 'because I found I was becoming a different person, a better person from when I started, and I was living a happier life than before. I went again to completely clarify all I was learning and found the extra sessions extremely beneficial. Now any time that I feel that I am losing the importance of these ideas I quickly go back to The Gawler Foundation to reinforce them.'

During 1985 Jim continued to look better and better. Urged to go for more tests and scans, Jim refused. Jim kept in touch with his doctors but as for detailed tests, he said: 'I don't want to know', his eyes closed and arms up in characteristic Greek fashion! 'I feel great. If the cancer is still there or worse, I don't want to know, I can't do any more and it's OK. If the cancer has gone, I still don't want to change any thing. I'm enjoying life. I could die tomorrow but I expect to live a long time again now.'

Finally in April 1986, Jim relented and had full tests conducted. 'I was very surprised and quite elated to find that there was no trace of it anywhere in my body.' A full remission when no medical treatment was available!

Jim continues to nurture his good health, maintaining his diet, meditation and positivity. He also acts as an inspiration to many via the voluntary contact group and often spends hours with other people and their families (especially Greeks) just starting on the road he has walked. It is wonderful to see him, giving so much of his experience to others.

June 1992—A Tribute to a Friend

Many members and friends of The Gawler Foundation will have been saddened by the news of Jim's death. While Jim's life was a miracle to celebrate, the fact that he is no longer walking amongst us, spreading his hope and good humour, is really saddening.

Jim was one of those exceptional beings who, having experienced a remarkable, medically unexpected recovery, marvelled at what happened for him and wanted to share the good news. He gave so much of himself in voluntary service, visiting those recently diagnosed in their homes or hospital, often calling on others in advanced illness. Always the same message: there is hope, you can help yourself, your family and friends can make a difference, life is worth living, make the effort, it will be repaid in full.

My guess is that some will be unsettled by Jim's death. He had come to be another prominent symbol of what is possible. That cancer can be overcome not only in living with it and being the better for the experience of it, but in actually recovering physically.

I know that Jim was concerned about this impact of his declining health and his death approaching. It was good to have been able to talk with him again a few days before he did die and remind him of his triumph. He survived some seven years longer than expected. He brought inspiration, hope and real health and peace to literally hundreds, perhaps thousands of others in real need. I told him how I had come to love him and how many others held him in their love.

Jim's was a great life, made greater by his response to the huge challenge presented by cancer and all he subsequently helped. Please pray for him and hold him dear in your heart during meditation. And offer your support to his wife Angela and the boys.

For those of us fortunate enough to know this man, Jim Malliaros' life was a miracle.

Ian Gawler
From Inspiring People, *The Gawler Foundation, 1995*
Used with permission.

Edward

The oldest amongst us;
he had reached his three-score
and ten some years before.
Gentle, well-spoken,
economical with his words.
Like a sage under sufferance
in this motley group.
Over forty years he'd seen
patients with this dreaded disease.
Unexpectedly, they discovered it in his kidneys,
with secondaries in the lung.
Fear had no place in his logic.

Like a Stoic he cursed the wretched thing.
Vowed to fight and win.
Within three days he smiled.
Within a week he laughed
at the diet they said
would help to fuel his recovery.
His beloved French cooking
consigned to wistful nostalgia.
Lustily lampooning each
vegetable juice (especially the green),
each buckwheat slice,
each ratatouille pie
(strictly vegetarian, of course),
each new form of meditation,
yet embracing all
with a zealot's zeal.

On his own admission
half a life ago
the last vestige
of stereotyped religion
disappeared.
Now, at eventide

with such candour
he yearned for
a spiritual renaissance,
a still small Voice
which might assuage,
perhaps resolve
puzzles which,
like an habitual
petty thief,
stole his peace of mind.

                                        Paul Kraus

DEATH AND DYING

Living and Dying Well

In his best-selling book *You Can Conquer Cancer*, Ian Gawler subtitles his chapter on death and dying, 'An integral part of living'. He writes: 'This book is about living, so it is about dying, too. Dying is a natural process. It is an integral part of life. We are going to experience it this lifetime. So you do not need a terminal illness to prepare for death.' (p. 160)

Death still tends to be regarded as one of those taboo subjects, much the same as sex was a taboo subject in Victorian England. Why? Primarily because of fear: fear of the unknown and also fear of the process of dying. However, I believe that there is another reason, namely, that we live in an age of unbelief—an age where belief in the material things of life has replaced any form of spirituality in people's lives. This is why so few people seem to have an awareness of themselves and the meaning of their existence.

One of Gawler's main arguments is that if we could only learn to live well, to live life to the full, enjoy living and learn to live without fear, then we would recognise that the techniques for living well are really synonymous with those of dying well.

The poems and extracts in this section illustrate healthy and positive emotions (including humour) about death and dying. They also illustrate the truth of Ian Gawler's idea that the art of death lies in the art of living.

If I Had My Life to Live Over

The following poem was written by an elderly American woman as she confronted her death. It is a remarkable piece of writing.

If I had my life to live over, I'd try
To make more mistakes next time, I would
Relax, I would limber up, I would be crazier
Than I've been on this trip. I know very
Few things I would take seriously any more.
Trips, I would scale more mountains,
I would swim more rivers, and I would
Watch more sunsets. I would eat more
Ice cream and fewer beans.
I would have more actual troubles
And fewer imaginary ones. You see ...
I was one of those people who lived
Prophylactically and sensibly and sanely,
Hour after hour and day after day ...
Oh, I've had my moments
And if I had to do it all over
Again, I'd have many more of them.
In fact, I'd try not to have anything
Else, just moments, one after another,
Instead of living so many
Years ahead of my day.
I've been one of those people
who never went anywhere without
A thermometer, a hot water bottle, a gargle, a
Raincoat and a parachute (and if she travelled with
Bobbie, a tape recorder, an iron and a hair dryer)
If I had to do it all over again,
I'd travel lighter, much lighter,
Than I have.
I would start barefoot earlier
In the Spring, and I'd stay that way
Later in the Fall. And I would

Ride more merry-go-rounds, and
Catch more gold rings and greet
More people, and pick more flowers,
And dance more often, if I had it
To do all over again.
But you see,
I don't.

Nadine Stair
Quoted from Love, Medicine and Miracles, *Bernie Siegel, MD*

Reflections

Death is nothing at all. I have only slipped away into the next room. I am I, and you are you. Whatever we were to each other, that we still are. Call me by my old familiar name. Speak to me in the same easy way which you always used. Put no difference in your tone, wear no forced air of solemnity or sorrow. Laugh as we always laughed at the little jokes we enjoyed together. Pray, smile, think of me, pray for me. Let my name be ever the household word it always was. Let it be spoken without effect, without the trace of a shadow on it.

Life means all that it ever meant. It is the same as it ever was; there is an unbroken continuity. Why should I be out of mind because I am out of sight? I am waiting for you, for an interval, somewhere very near ... just around the corner.

All is well.

Canon Henry Scott Holland, 1847–1918
Dean of St Paul's Cathedral, London

Is It Possible to Die in a Healed Condition?

Why not? Death and healing are not opposites. To die as a healed person would mean being able to view one's life as complete and accept the disintegration of the physical body. There are many reliable accounts of the last days of sages, especially from Buddhist traditions and extending up to the present day, that illustrate the possibility of healing into death. They bear little resemblance to what goes on in modern hospitals, where doctors often see death as the ultimate enemy to be fought with all the weapons of modern medical technology. Trapped on this battle ground, patients usually have no opportunity for final healing, nor do people in our culture have ready access to practical information about using life to prepare for death. In other cultures and in other times, 'the art of dying' was a popular theme of books and discourse. I would like to see it revived.

Extract from Spontaneous Healing, *by Andrew Weil, MD*
The Ballantine Publishing Group,
(A Division of Random House) New York, 1996.
Used with permission.

Death is a Part of Life

An old Hasidic tale tells how the angels weep when a soul enters a physical body at birth and how they rejoice when it returns to the heavenly realms at death. This is a very different way of looking at life, isn't it? We usually think of our lives as straight lines beginning with birth and ending at death—the longer the line the better. In Native American tradition, in contrast, life is thought of as a circle. Whether the circle is small or large, death marks its completion rather than destruction. Yet, death is part of the wholeness of life. There is an ancient story which illustrates this thought and helps us to understand why some people's lives are cut short in the prime of life:

Before Siddharta Gautama became the Buddha, he was a young prince supplied with every conceivable luxury. His father had gone to great lengths to keep him inside the palace, protected from exposure to suffering. One day the curious prince demanded that his charioteer take him into the city. Spying a sick person, he inquired, 'What is that?' His charioteer explained that all human flesh was heir to illness. Next he asked about a very old man, hobbling with a cane. Once again, the charioteer explained that all flesh had to age. Finally, Siddharta saw a corpse burning on a funeral pyre. Stunned, he asked whether that would happen to him and his family as well. Once again, the charioteer pointed out the impermanence of the human body.

The future Buddha was so distressed that he left the palace and took up the life of a renunciate holy man, vowing to find an end to suffering. The method that the Buddha eventually taught, following his enlightenment, did not obliterate sickness, old age, or death. Neither was it about using the power of your mind to manifest wealth or to win friends and influence people. Liberation was not about the body or about filling our endless desires. It was about attaining a state of peace, joy, wisdom, and compassion that was not dependent on any outside condition . . .

The Buddha's message is as powerful today as it was 2,500 years ago. But we have to have the ears to hear it. Perhaps the saddest misunderstanding of the power of the mind to heal is the twisting of the Buddha's message. Rather than transcending suffering, which means that we must learn and grow from it, the 'New Age' message is that we can eliminate it. Just think right and you can cure illness, prevent aging, and possibly even live in your current body for hundreds of years, some New Agers offer. Perhaps at death you can even ascend, leaving a little pile of hair and fingernails. A few mystics have done just that, but by far, the greater majority have died of cancer and other diseases, often at young ages. Can we reasonably assume that these great masters were psychological basket cases or spiritual failures? The Buddha himself died of food poisoning, but not before explaining to the cook that his time here was done and he needed a doorway out of his body! . . .

When we make perfect bodies the focus of our lives, we will inevitably be very disappointed. While we need to do what we can both to stay well and to cure our illness when possible, a total healing is not always our destiny . . . Too often we've been taught to think that poverty or illness is a divine punishment, or at least our 'bad karma' returning to us . . . when in reality some life events are actually soul contracts that we agreed to for our own or someone else's benefit . . . Can you imagine that a person's serious illness may in fact be a gift, an act of service, that helps other people toward a more compassionate awareness?

Extract taken from The Power of the Mind to Heal
by Joan and Miroslav Borysenko
(Australian edition, 1995).
Used with the permission of the publisher,
Specialist Publications, Concord, NSW.

Psalm 23—The Lord as Shepherd and Protector in Life and Death

The Lord is my shepherd, I shall lack nothing;
He makes me down to lie in green pastures,
He leads me beside still waters;
He restores my soul.
He leads me in paths of righteousness for His name's sake.
Even though I walk through the valley of the shadow of
    death, I fear no evil,
for You are with me; Your presence comforts me.
You prepare a table before me in the presence of my enemies;
You anoint my head with oil,
My cup overflows.
Surely goodness and mercy shall follow me
all the days of my life
and I shall dwell in the house of the Lord forever.

Our Victory Over Death—The Letter of Paul to the Romans 8: 28, 35-39

We know that in everything God works for good, with those who love Him, who are called according to His purpose.

... Who shall separate us from the love of Christ?

Shall tribulation, or distress, or famine, or nakedness, or peril, or even death itself?

... No, in all these things we are more than conquerors through Him who loved us. For I am sure that neither death, nor life, nor angels nor principalities, nor things present, nor things to come, nor powers, nor height, nor anything else in all creation will be able to separate us from the love of God ...

Excerpts taken from The Holy Bible, *Revised Standard Version*
Thomas Nelson, London, 1959.

On Living and Dying

Elisabeth Kubler-Ross, a Swiss-American psychiatrist, began her pioneering work with dying patients in the USA in the 1960s. Her work has been documented in the many books she has written, beginning with On Death and Dying *(1969) which became a classic in its field. Her last book was her autobiography,* The Wheel of Life *(1997). One of her basic ideas, which comes through in all her writings, is that it is only when we are able to face up to our own mortality, that we are able to live fully and lovingly. More than any other writer on the subject of death and dying, Elisabeth Kubler-Ross has articulated the nexus between the way we live and the way we die. At the end of her autobiography she writes:*

> Dying is nothing to fear. It can be the most wonderful experience of your life. It all depends on how you have lived. Death is but a transition from this life to another existence where there is no more pain and anguish. Everything is bearable when there is love. My wish is that you try to give more people love. The only thing that lives forever is love.

Kubler-Ross quotes a beautiful poem about love and the meaning of life written by an old man for his children and grandchildren.

When you love, give it everything you have got.
And when you have reached your limit, give it more,
and forget the pain of it.
Because as you face your death
it is only the love you have given and received
which will count,
and all the rest:
the accomplishments, the struggle, the fights
will be forgotten in your reflection.
And if you have loved well
then it will all have been worth it.
And the joy of it will last you through the end.
But if you have not,

death will always come too soon
and be too terrible to face.

The following extract appears on the back cover of her autobiography and represents Kubler-Ross' understanding of death. Her words are characterised by their simplicity and beauty.

When we have passed the tests we were sent to earth to learn, we are allowed to graduate. We are allowed to shed our body, which imprisons our soul the way a cocoon encloses the future butterfly, and when the time is right we can let go of it. Then we will be free of pain, free of fears and free of worries ... free as a beautiful butterfly returning home to God ... which is a place where we are never alone, where we continue to grow and to sing and to dance, where we are with those we loved and where we are surrounded with more love than we can ever imagine.

Dr Elisabeth Kubler-Ross, 1997.
Extracted from The Wheel of Life,
published by Bantam Press,
a division of Transworld Publishers Ltd.

Dying Isn't the Worst Outcome: How to Survive Living or Dying

In the following extract Dr Bernie Siegel beautifully illustrates the idea that, in the final analysis, we can be healed without necessarily being cured of our physical symptoms. Death, that great source of fear for so many, can be a wonderful experience, not a tragedy. Everything depends on how we have lived, on how much we have given, on what our goals and desires have been.

One of our cancer therapy groups was discussing life, death and all the problems we have in between. Everyone in the room had problems, and as we talked about them one after another, we all worried about how they would turn out. It was getting depressing until finally one member said, 'Dying isn't the worst outcome'. Our laughter didn't make our problems go away but it ended our complaining.

On another occasion the same group was pondering the fears and the difficulties of the process of dying when one group member said, 'I can survive dying'. Again, the laughter healed us . . .

If living is difficult, dying will be too. If you live a life of love, service, faith and peace, your death will be a peaceful one. If your life is filled with regret, desire, fear and anger, your death will be difficult. Some people have a difficult time dying because they feel they have failed their family and don't have their permission to die. If you have lived a full life, are tired of your body and want to leave, you don't need anyone's permission. But if you live a life others choose for you, you'll need their permission to die.

Those who have lived authentic lives, defined by their choices, desires and uniqueness, have a different experience with death. They are full of life to their last moment and die without any difficulties, surrounded by loved ones. Those are good deaths. I do not mean to disregard the grief a family feels. Death is a loss to the living. But some people live so successfully that when it is time to die they simply exercise their freedom to leave a body that is too tired for them to love with. For them, death is a time to turn the set off. Leaving their body is their next treatment. It is a spiritual therapy.

Extract taken from pp. 130–131 of Prescriptions for Living *by*
Bernie Siegel, MD
Rider, Random House, London, 1999.
Used with permission.

A Holy Moment

The following poem represents a Christian perspective on the moment of death—a moment in which we are 'born to eternal life'. This is a gift, the Christian believes, which Christ gained through His death and resurrection, thus once and for all destroying our need to fear death. St Paul expressed this fact so succinctly when he wrote 'that the perishable will put on the imperishable, and the mortal puts on immortality'.

When striving ceases, when ego dies,
when only praise and alleluias rise,
when I awake on Resurrection's morn,
when I shall glimpse that glorious dawn.

Then shall I see my Master's face
and stand in His amazing grace.
Unceasing love forever free—
it is this Lord who died for me.

A holy moment that will be,
sheer ecstasy to be set free
from tyranny of self; from fear
and doubt; anxiety ever near.

A holy moment that will be,
to meet the angels and to see
loved ones from this veil of tears,
there to dwell beyond all years.

No more hunger, no more thirst,
then the last shall be the first,
then this puzzling tapestry—
profound in its eternity.

A holy moment that will be!

Paul Kraus

SUFFERING

The Meaning of Suffering

A book such as this, dealing with health and healing, would be incomplete without a section on suffering—a topic mentioned in the introduction and alluded to in several poems and short stories in this collection.

What follows are two perspectives on the meaning of suffering. They both express much the same message, although in quite different ways. The first extract is from a chapter on suffering in former ABC journalist Caroline Jones' book, *An Authentic Life: Finding Meaning and Spirituality in Everyday Life*. The central theme of this passage is that, while suffering is a universal human experience, it can be imbued with meaning and the gaining of wisdom. This is particularly the case when we realise that suffering can actually be ennobling and bring us not only to a greater understanding of the vulnerability of the human condition, but also a greater awareness of our interdependence on one another as we go along life's journey.

The second was written in the 1960s by a survivor of the Holocaust and the Auschwitz death camp, Dr Viktor Frankl, who subsequently became a world-famous psychiatrist. In *Man's Search for Meaning* Frankl argues that while suffering is of course unavoidable, the challenge of suffering is the meaning we extract from it and the way we live out that suffering.

An Authentic Life

One of the most important aspects of life to come to terms with is suffering. Yet we do everything to avoid it. Earlier generations may have had a more realistic acceptance of the integral place of suffering in life, but in modern Western society the prevailing message is that suffering can be anaesthetised with fun, sex, excitement, drugs, alcohol, taking risks, shopping, the amassing of information, or overwork; or ended with suicide or euthanasia. This carries the assumption that the only proper goal in life is pleasure—that suffering is an aberration. Armed with this misunderstanding, we venture into the world ill-equipped to deal with setbacks and missing the point of human experience altogether. To find some coherent and hopeful way to deal with suffering is one of the crucial keys to a life of meaning ...

Paradoxical as it is, suffering often brings out the nobility in us ... There are many people living faithful, unsung and sometimes desperate lives of devotion caring for frail or incapacitated relatives or friends. Most of these things are done privately and we may think they make little difference in the grand scheme of things. But every such action has its own intrinsic worth. It is something of lasting and ultimate importance, whether it is acknowledged or not. Whatever you may do to bear your own suffering with hope or to alleviate the suffering of others is an encouraging inspiration to those around you. In a way that is often hard to see, it nurtures the spiritual life of the giver, the recipient and the whole community.

Gradually, through experience, we may learn that almost every episode of suffering is not only painful but also maturing: that it takes us to a new stage of understanding and leaves us with more resources and courage than we had before, often with more wisdom. This is a significant insight that we need to take in and carry with us. Then it becomes a sustaining inner knowledge that an upset is not an impasse, but an experience with various layers of testing, some of which contain the possibilities of personal growth ...

One approach to suffering is to decide what, for you, constitutes a good life. Does life have some intrinsic purpose? Is it perhaps a journey of learning, or does it have no aim but the maximisation of pleasure and the minimisation of pain? . . . A society like ours, which is frightened of illness and death, does not want to be confronted with its own frailty or mortality. We do not want to be reminded that, in spite of the many triumphs of science, illness and death have not been conquered, and that they will come to each of us. In a society that prizes personal autonomy we are fearful of the dependence that suffering may bring, yet the reality is that we are dependent on each other all through life, in many ways. My every action and decision impinges on those around me, as their decisions and actions affect my life. That is the way it is, yet so often we insist on the illusion of our independence, preferring denial to the truth . . .

A common view in western society to-day is that I 'own' my life, and therefore I control my life, and it is my right to make decisions and choices accordingly . . . The autonomous view of life is fostered especially in men who are rewarded for independent toughness and competitiveness. Suffering of any kind may be especially difficult for the person who holds this belief because it forces him to realise that everything is not, after all, under his control. The experience may shake him to the foundations because it reveals a vulnerability he had denied. He may experience it as a humiliating weakness . . . Taken to an extreme, he may even opt to end his own life rather than submit to the process of suffering. On the other hand, if he can submit to it, he may be changed by that humbling experience of dependence to see that he does indeed need help from others, that they are willing to give it to him, and that the acceptance of their help has some unexpected rewards . . .

Another view of life is that it is a gift from God and that our role is to co-operate with God in the unfolding of our destiny, even when that includes suffering. This does not mean that God inflicts suffering but that, however difficult things become, there is a purpose in life that only God can know fully, and one has faith in that purpose even when it seems inexplicable. This is a less lonely framework in which to encounter suffering

169

than that of the person who holds personal autonomy as the highest value ...

It is important to think about suffering because it comes to us all, and our ideas about it give us a basis on which to start to deal with it, both as individuals and as citizens of a humane society. However, there are many complexities and subtleties in this peculiarly challenging aspect of life. Each person's suffering is unique and all the thinking we do about it will be tempered by the actual experience of it, in our own lives and in the lives of those around us.

Caroline Jones, An Authentic Life
ABC Books, Sydney, 1998.
Reproduced with permission.

The Mystery of Suffering

The darker the night
    of suffering,
the more radiant
the life of pure love
    that
emerges from it.

C. de Foucauld

I shall lead you
    through
        the loneliness,
the solitude
you will not understand;
but it is My shortcut
to your soul.

Thomas Merton

The Meaning of Suffering

Whenever one is confronted with an inescapable, unavoidable situation, whenever one has to face a fate that cannot be changed, e.g. an incurable disease, such as an inoperable cancer, just then one is given a last chance to actualise the highest value, to fulfil the deepest meaning, the meaning of suffering. For what matters above all is the attitude we take toward suffering, the attitude in which we take our suffering upon ourselves . . .

It goes without saying that suffering would not have meaning unless it were absolutely necessary; e.g. a cancer that can be cured by surgery must not be shouldered by the patient as though it were his cross. This would be masochism rather than heroism . . .

There are situations in which one is cut off from the opportunity to do one's work or to enjoy one's life; but what can never be ruled out is the unavoidability of suffering. In accepting this challenge to suffer bravely, life has a meaning up to the last moment, and it retains this meaning literally to the end. In other words, life's meaning is an unconditional one, for it even includes the potential meaning of suffering.

Let me recall that which was perhaps the deepest experience I had in the concentration camp. The odds of surviving the camp were no more than one to twenty-eight, as can be verified by exact statistics. It did not even seem possible, let alone probable, that the manuscript of my first book, which I had hidden in my coat when I arrived in Auschwitz, would ever be rescued. Thus, I had to undergo and to overcome the loss of my spiritual child. And now it seemed as if nothing and no one would survive me; neither a physical nor a spiritual child of my own! So I found myself confronted with the question of whether under such circumstances my life was void of any meaning.

Not yet did I notice that an answer to this question with which I was wrestling so passionately was already in store for me, and that soon thereafter this answer would be given to me. This was the case when I had to surrender my clothes and in turn inherit the worn-out rags of an inmate who had been sent to the gas chamber immediately after his arrival at the Auschwitz railway station. Instead of the many pages of my manuscript, I found in a pocket of the newly acquired coat a single page torn out of a Hebrew prayer book, which contained the main Jewish prayer, Shema Yisrael. How should I have interpreted such a 'coincidence' other than as a challenge to *live* my thoughts instead of merely putting them on paper?

A bit later, I remember, it seemed to me that I would die in the near future. In this critical situation, however, my concern was different from that of most of my comrades. Their question was, 'Will we survive the camp? For, if not, all this suffering has no meaning.' The question which beset me was, 'Has all this suffering, this dying around us, a meaning? For, if not, then ultimately there is no meaning to survival; for a life whose meaning depends upon such a circumstance—whether one escapes or not—ultimately would not be worth living at all.'

Viktor Frankl, Man's Search for Meaning
Pocket Books, Beacon Press, New York, 1963.
Reproduced with permission.

REMARKABLE
RECOVERIES

Towards a New Medicine

Miracles do not happen in contradiction of nature, but in contradiction of what we know about nature.

St Augustine

Cases of remarkable recovery are inspiring human sagas, priceless raw material, sources of information and hope, and new clues to the healing process. But they are also an impetus and, in some way, a blueprint for the remarkable recovery of the medical system itself. There is today a grassroots movement to bind the wounds between hard and soft sciences, between the ill and their caregivers; to forge a new medicine focused as much on the potential of the whole person as on the potency of the treatment. It is no longer far-fetched to envision a new science of spirit and values working hand in hand with biology and technology to create a new patient-centred medicine, one focused more on wellness than illness ...

To come to grips with the mystery—and the reality—of remarkable recovery calls for a new conceptual framework, new research techniques, and most certainly, a fresh set of questions. If there are larger patterns—any patterns—associated with the disappearance or arrest of a tumour, they would suggest new, multi-pronged programmes of prevention and treatment. In the course of our journey (of documenting remarkable recoveries), our healing system 'checklist' has swelled to dozens of synergistic factors. But it is unknown how many items would need to be checked off in a particular case—how many factors, in other words, are needed to kickstart the healing system?

Some researchers would maintain that the question is an oxymoron—that there *is* no healing system to kickstart; that remarkable recoveries are random statistical anomalies with no discernible cause; and that a handful of anomalies do not call for any change in the practice of medicine. Writes Yale radiologist Richard Peschel:

Scientific miracles are very rare and science does not—and does not have to—try to explain them. This may seem strange to a lay person, but it is enough for the scientist to know that extremely unlikely events do occur, that they *have* to occur, in fact, because they are statistically possible. Thus scientific miracles do not need any explanation.

This suggestion makes the assumption that each case of remarkable recovery is a 'unique experiment of nature'. But the study of the possible influence of moods and emotions, personality traits, social support, beliefs and attitudes lobs a quiet bombshell into the settled precincts of experimental medicine: can we ever be certain whether 'real' treatment does not owe an unknown portion of its curative power to these 'non-medical' factors? For that matter, how can we know the extent to which mind–body factors might account for the successes of even ostensibly well-proven treatments? . . . Because a treatment is considered to be conventional and accepted does not necessarily imply that it is proven or specific. The thin line between applied scientific medicine and the power of the doctor–patient relationship is highly permeable. In clinical practice, they may become indistinguishable . . .

Controlled, randomised drug studies ignore psychological, social and spiritual factors. Until we know—and take into account—how varying states of mind, degrees of suggestibility, psychoneuroimmunological responsiveness, individual health practices, attitudes . . . and even religious experiences affect the progress or regression of disease, it is hard to have unbending faith in the results of experiments that never posed the questions.

The extent to which individual differences are not taken into account in both the study and promotion of the healing response is not only detrimental to the healer's art, but a challenge to the scientific method itself . . .

Doctors Jeanne Achterberg and Frank Lawlis, principal investigators for the National Cancer Institute grants have said:

Randomised control group designs have not and simply cannot

yield satisfactory answers in complex behavioural or psycho-social studies with human beings ... to let a research methodology dictate the design and nature of the research question (instead of the other way around) is an aberration of the scientific method. The tail, quite plainly, is wagging the dog ...

The issue of just how much psychoemotional factors affect patient health has been rocking almost violently back and forth in what might be perceived as the birth pangs of a new medical paradigm ...

Extract taken from Remarkable Recovery:
What Extraordinary Healings Can Teach Us About Getting Well and Staying Well *by Carle Hirschberg*
and Marc Ian Barasch
Headline Book Publishing, London, 1995.
Used with permission.

A Prayer for Healing

Lord, be our Healing.
Give us complete confidence
in your power to heal in
the way You know it needs to take place.
Help us to work in harmony with
You, not against You.

Remove from us
all that obstructs Your loving
power to heal. In place of anger, hurt,
bitterness, failure to forgive,
fill us with Love, Joy, Peace,
Patience, Kindness, Goodness,
Faithfulness, Gentleness
and Self-Control.

Let these growing in us
be the signs of our healing.
Amen.

Acknowledgements

All references from the Bible are from the Revised Standard Version published by Thomas Nelson and Sons, Ltd, Edinburgh, 1957; Alfred A Knopf, Inc for excerpt from *Spontaneous Healing*, by Andrew Weil, MD; 'Suffering,' reproduced from *An Authentic Life* by Caroline Jones, ABC Books; the poem 'Convalescence' by Peter Skrzynecki from *Easter Sunday* with permission of HarperCollins Publishers; Hill of Content Publishing Melbourne for permission to reproduce extracts from *Dialogue on Meditation*, from *The Quiet Place*, and *A Kind of Believing* by Ainslie Meares; Specialist Publications, Sydney, for extracts from *The Power of the Mind to Heal* by Joan Borysenko; HarperCollins Publishers for extracts from *Living, Loving and Healing* by Bernie Siegel, MD; Hodder Headline, London, for the extract from *Remarkable Recovery* by Carle Hirschberg and Marc Barasch; Transworld Publishers, London, for permission to reproduce material from *The Wheel of Life: A Memoir of Living and Dying* by Elisabeth Kubler-Ross; Simon and Schuster, New York (Pocket Book imprint) for permission to extract from *Man's Search for Meaning* by Viktor Frankl; The Gawler Foundation for permission to reproduce the extract from *Inspiring People*; The Humour Foundation for their co-operation in supplying photographs.

The author would like to thank Dr Heather Cam for her consummate editorial skills in transforming a rough manuscript into a fine book. Gratitude also to Bert Hingley of Hale and Iremonger for his help and encouragement from the very beginning of this project.

Every effort has been made to contact copyright holders. The publisher would like to hear from any copyright holder where unintentional infringement has resulted from copyright proving untraceable.

The Humour Foundation

The Humour Foundation was incorporated in January 1997. The Clown Doctor Unit was established at Sydney Childrens' Hospital, Randwick, in January 1997 and at the Royal Childrens' Hospital, Melbourne, in February 1997.

International research has demonstrated the physiological and psychological benefits of humour. The value of humour is widely recognised by health professionals and is part of a worldwide trend. The Clown Doctors visit children in hospital. Using their skills of improvisation, magic, music, mime and juggling, they treat young patients with doses of fun and fantasy. The emphasis is on interaction, rather than on entertainment. Each child's situation is different, and the approach is adapted to suit each case. The performers are adaptable and flexible, always taking their cue from the patient. Empowerment of the child is important in a situation where they have little control.

Clown Doctors parody the hospital routine and exaggerate intimidating jargon and procedures to humorous extremes, helping to reduce fear and anxiety. Clown Doctors work in partnership with hospital staff towards a patient's recovery or palliative care.

Clown Doctors also work with the families of patients to help reduce their stress and anxiety. The anticipated outcomes include: helping children to deal with loneliness and isolation and helping them (together with their carers and families) to maintain a positive outlook.

The Humour Foundation aims to establish Clown Doctor units in major hospitals throughout Australia by the end of the year 2000.

Donations to help make this aim a reality can be forwarded to the Humour Foundation, P.O. Box 5, Avalon Beach, NSW 2107. All donations are fully tax deductible. You can also contact the Foundation on the Internet website: http://www.fiddlybytes.com.au/humourfoundation